M000024624

WHO KNEW?

THE BIG BOOK OF QUESTIONS THAT WILL MAKE YOU THINK AGAIN

Sarah Herman

PORTABLE
PRESS

San Diego, California

Portable Press
An imprint of Printers Row Publishing Group
9717 Pacific Heights Blvd, San Diego, CA 92121
www.portablepress.com • mail@portablepress.com

Copyright © 2021 Quarto Publishing plc

All rights reserved. No part of this publication may be reproduced, distributed, or transmitted in any form or by any means, including photocopying, recording, or other electronic or mechanical methods, without the prior written permission of the publisher, except in the case of brief quotations embodied in critical reviews and certain other noncommercial uses permitted by copyright law.

Printers Row Publishing Group is a division of Readerlink Distribution Services, LLC. Portable Press is a registered trademark of Readerlink Distribution Services, LLC.

This edition contains text previously published by © 2017 Quarto Publishing plc.

Correspondence regarding the content of this book should be sent to Portable Press, Editorial Department, at the above address. Author and illustration inquiries should be addressed to The Bright Press, part of The Quarto Group, Level 1, Ovest House, 58 West Street, Brighton, UK, BN1 2RA.

Portable Press
Publisher: Peter Norton
Associate Publisher: Ana Parker
Editor: Dan Mansfield
Acquisitions Editor: Kathryn Chipinka Dalby

Conceived and designed by The Bright Press, part of The Quarto Group, The Old Brewery, 6 Blundell Street, London, N7 9BH

Cover and page design: Lindsey Johns
Text: Sarah Herman

ISBN: 978-1-64517-687-9

Library of Congress Control Number: 2021931043

Printed in Singapore

25 24 23 22 21 1 2 3 4 5

"For Ian, for always keeping me guessing!"

CONTENTS

INTRODUCTION

There's nothing quite like being the biggest brainiac in the boardroom, the dinner party guest who really shows their knowledge, the office buddy who chimes in to settle an argument, or the parent who always has the last word around the dinner table.

Having the facts at your fingertips is one thing, but being able to explain who, what, where, and why puts you a step above those quick-fire quizmasters. This book is all about expanding your mind and fueling you with the answers to curious questions, many of which you might never have thought to ask. And all of which will leave you exclaiming, "Who knew?"

Over the following chapters you'll get to grips with wild weather, bodily functions, outstanding artworks, and mind-boggling botanicals. You'll travel back in time to the lands of the ancients, read up on the lives of authors, and don your protective goggles for some good old-fashioned science. And if all that's not enough, take a trip around the world, get clued up on the origins of sports (whiff-whaff, anyone?), and arrive at the outer reaches of the galaxy.

From the silly ("Is Michelangelo's David based on David Schwimmer?") and the scientific ("Is the periodic table complete?") to the unusual ("What happened to the Soviet space dogs?") and the unexpected ("What did Vladimir Nabokov keep in his cabinet?"), you'll soon be an expert on the clever and bizarre spectrum that *Who Knew?* covers. You'll be the one exhibiting your latest learnings by the water cooler and wowing your friends and family with tidbits of tantalizing trivia.

Of course, all this reading is no good without retention. That's why, at the end of each section, there's a quick quiz to keep you on your toes. Test yourself and your friends with these pithy pickings from each chapter to make sure you know more than they do. You'll soon realize that while money and accolades are nice, knowledge (and being a smug smarty-pants) really is its own reward.

So get ready to galvanize your gray matter and sharpen your *savoir faire* as you step into the wondrous world of knowing it all—or, at the very least, knowing a lot more than you did before.

WEATHER
AND CLIMATE

1 WHAT TURNS COASTAL WATERS INTO COFFEE?

Australia is known for its coffee culture—three-quarters of the population have at least one cup a day—but in 2007 the caffeine-crazy country took coffee to a whole new level.

NEXT-LEVEL LATTE ART

Rare coastal conditions transformed part of the New South Wales shore into a foamy spectacle. Ocean foam of epic proportions, stretching 150 feet out to sea, swallowed up cars, lifeguard stations, and engulfed the bottom halves of beachside homes, lasting for days. Locals lathered themselves frolicking on the beach, and some keen surfers even took to the waves. The frothy, coffee-colored foam gave the area its nickname: "Cappuccino Coast."

FROTHY COFFEE CONDITIONS

Unsurprisingly, this unusual phenomenon is not the result of a coffee-carrying tanker spill. It's caused when impurities in the oceans, like algae, plant and animal material, chemicals, and salts, are tossed and churned by ocean currents and stormy weather conditions. The organic material acts as a surfactant—similarly to dish detergent, these substances lower the surface tension of water molecules, causing little bubbles to form. The bubbles get trapped under the surface, and the choppy waves act like a running tap frothing up the water. As the bubbles slowly make their way to the shore, clinging together, the soft foam is created.

SALTWATER COFFEE?

While the salty seawater on the "Cappuccino Coast" definitely wasn't for drinking, in Hungary, Siberia, Turkey, and some Scandinavian countries, salty coffee is a tradition. The sodium ion is thought to reduce coffee's bitter taste for a better all-around flavor.

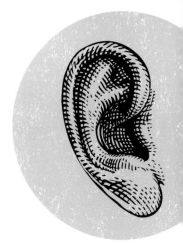

2 CAN YOU TELL THE TEMPERATURE WITH YOUR EARS?

We humans rely on technology to tell us just how hot or cold it is, but there's another lesser-known method to figure out the temperature: listening to crickets.

COLD-BLOODED CHIRPS

In 1897, American physicist and inventor Amos Dolbear published an article in *The American Naturalist* titled "The cricket as a thermometer." What Dolbear realized is that the cold-blooded cricket matches the temperature of its surroundings, and that the number of chirps it produces increases the warmer it is. Crickets have scrapers on their wings and rub one across the underside of the other wing, in a process called stridulation, to make that distinctive sound.

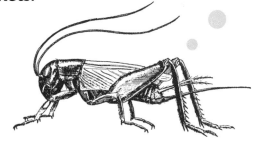

between species—it's thought Dolbear observed the snowy tree cricket—as a 1930 issue of *Science* talking about the discovery commented: "Every individual cricket, like every clock or watch, must be regarded as a specific mechanism with specific modes of behavior."

THE LAW OF CHIRPING

Known as Dolbear's Law, it's easy to convert cricket chirps into degrees Fahrenheit. Just count the number of chirps you hear in 14 seconds and then add 40 to get the temperature. If you prefer Celsius, count the number of chirps in 25 seconds, divide that by three, and then add four. Voilà! You've told the temperature with your ears. The rate of chirps varies

BROOKS'S LAW?

The law might have been named for him, but Dolbear was not the first to publish on the matter. Margarette W. Brooks of Salem, Massachusetts, was the first to mention this phenomenon in a scientific magazine, although her work has largely gone unrecognized.

3 HOW FAST CAN A SAND DUNE MOVE?

From Marco Polo and Alexander the Great to Genghis Khan and Gertrude Bell, some of the world's most famous adventurers, conquerors, and explorers have traveled across deserts to change the course of history. But you might not know that the sand dunes are traveling, too, at the mercy of the winds.

CARRIED AWAY

Sand dunes are formed when there's an abundance of sand, strong wind, and shrubs or rocks that obstruct the sand so it piles up. There are three ways that sand moves: suspension, creeping, and saltation. Suspension—when a sand grain is blown high into the air by a very strong wind—accounts for only about 1 percent of sand dunes' movement. And creeping accounts for about 4 percent.

BOUNCING ALONG

Saltation is the predominant cause of movement and occurs when the wind lifts the grains a few inches above the ground and drops them a couple of inches away, causing them to bounce and be lifted again.

As the sand builds up on the windward side of a dune, gravity takes hold and the grains at the top eventually fall over the other side, either as a trickle or in small avalanches. Eventually the whole face of the dune will collapse.

THE SANDS OF TIME

How quickly the dune moves depends on the wind speed, the dune's size, and the amount of vegetation in its path. Smaller dunes—those less than 20 feet high—are formed from less sand, so they move much more quickly and can travel as much as 40 feet per year. Some dunes in Great Sand Dune National Park in Colorado, where wind speeds reach 40 miles per hour, have been known to move around 3 feet per week. Barchan dunes—identified by their crescent moon shape—measure 30 to 100 feet high and over 1,200 feet wide, and typically move up to 12 feet per year. They're commonly found in open inland regions, including Turkestan and the Namib Desert.

FIVE QUICK FACTS

1 EARTH CAN BE VERY COLD

You need some thick socks and thermals if you plan on living in Oymyakon in Russia—the world's coldest permanently inhabited place, where the lowest temperature recorded is −90°F.

2 IT'S ALWAYS RAINING SOMEWHERE

Every year our planet experiences about 16 million thunderstorms, which means at any time about 2,000 are taking place around the world.

3 BEING BURIED IN THE SAND IS NO LAUGHING MATTER

An entire army of 50,000 Persian soldiers, fighting for King Cambyses in 525 BC, were trekking across Egypt's Western Desert when they were annihilated by a powerful sandstorm and buried where they stood.

4 FAITH IN FEATHERS

In the ninth century, Pope Nicholas I decreed that weather vanes shaped like roosters be placed on every church steeple as a symbol of St. Peter's denial of Jesus Christ.

5 WHERE WEATHER HAPPENS

Weather forms in the lowest layer of Earth's atmosphere, known as the troposphere. It's where 99 percent of the atmosphere's water vapor is too.

4 WHAT'S THE HEAVIEST THING A TORNADO CAN CARRY?

The United States experiences on average 1,000 tornadoes each year, a large percentage occurring in Tornado Alley in the south-central states. Tornadoes can be extremely powerful, causing tremendous damage, but due to their unpredictability and often remote locations, many go undocumented. When they are spotted, they can be hard to measure.

HOW DO TORNADOES FORM?

Tornadoes are the result of a convective "supercell" thunderstorm—an organized storm that contains a strong, rotating updraft. Tornadoes form inside the storm when warm, moist air on the ground converges with cool, drier air farther up that's moving in the opposite direction. This is known as wind shear and produces a spinning tube of air. This speeds up inside the storm, creating a funnel cloud, which then descends to the ground in a vertical tube. With the right conditions, tornadoes can pick up so much air, dirt, and debris that they can grow to a mile wide. The fastest tornadoes can move at speeds of more than 60 miles per hour, with wind speeds inside a tornado believed to be up to 318 miles per hour.

HEAVY LIFTERS

In *The Wonderful Wizard of Oz*, a tornado whisked up Dorothy's farmhouse and all its contents; in real life, the larger items that tornadoes can carry tend to be vehicles. Updraft suction and vertical velocity near the tornado's core help to pick up these large objects, and it's not unusual for them to carry 3,000-pound vans.

FAR, FAR AWAY

Small objects get swept up into tornadoes all the time. While they might not be as impressive in stature as a car or a truck, they can travel a lot farther. In 1995, University of Oklahoma researchers started studying the pattern of debris deposited by tornadoes. Over five years, they were sent more than 1,000 objects whose origin location could be identified, such as a bowling jacket with the owner's name stenciled on the back. Most of the objects had traveled 15 to 20 miles, but the farthest was 150 miles.

However, in 1990 a tornado in southwestern Texas was feeling greedy and managed to move three oil tanks around 3 miles east of their production facility. They are estimated to have weighed a total of 180,000 pounds. This is believed to be the heaviest thing a tornado has carried.

TWISTER TURMOIL

Fortunately, most tornadoes do not result in death. Advanced weather warning systems mean communities are often given sufficient notice to move out of a tornado's path or take shelter. The largest number of fatalities from a single tornado occurred in 1925, when 695 people from Missouri, Indiana, and Illinois died, while 2,027 were injured. In more recent years, in 2011, one of the deadliest tornadoes struck the city of Joplin, Missouri, killing 158 and injuring over 1,000. The terrifying twister reached wind speeds of 200 miles per hour.

5 HOW BIG CAN HAILSTONES GET?

From mini marbles to gargantuan grapefruits, hailstones of mythic proportions have long been the marvel of weather enthusiasts. But how do they form in the first place, and how big can they actually get?

HEAD IN THE CLOUDS

If you're a hailstone hunter, you might want to familiarize yourself with the cumulonimbus cloud. They start as tall, vertical formations, and it's their shape that helps create the perfect conditions

for a hailstorm to occur. As the conditions for rain begin to brew, the top part of the cloud flattens out, building up energy and getting ready to burst.

RAINY ROLLER COASTER

Typically, when water vapor in a cloud is cooled suddenly, it turns to ice crystals and falls to earth as snow. But cumulonimbus clouds are different. While the base of the cloud is warm and toasty, the temperature at the top can be well below freezing. This, combined with a strong updraft, sends falling raindrops from the lower level back up to the top, where they freeze. The frozen raindrops descend once again, start to thaw, collect more rain droplets, and then get sent back to the freezing heights of the cloud. This process occurs over and over until the weight of the frozen raindrop causes it to fall from the cloud: a hailstone is born.

SIZE MATTERS

All of this pinging up and down a cumulonimbus can lead to some pretty big hailstones. In 2010, a hailstone that fell on Vivian, South Dakota, was recorded as having a circumference of 18.625 inches and weighing in at 1.9375 pounds. Despite being the country's heaviest, it missed the circumference record of 18.75 inches, recorded in Aurora, Nebraska, seven years earlier.

The heaviest recorded hailstone in the world fell from the skies in 1986 over the Gopalganj area of Bangladesh. It weighed 2 pounds and was part of a deadly storm that killed 92 people. Sadly, India was no stranger to dangerous hailstorms, being the site of history's deadliest. In 1888, 248 people were killed after hailstones as large as baseballs rained down on Moradabad in Uttar Pradesh.

SEEDING THE STORM

After facing huge insurance payouts in 1991 after a ferocious 30-minute hailstorm, the insurance companies in Calgary, Canada, hired an aerospace business to keep future storms at bay. The process, known as seeding, sees planes fly above the potential hailstorm clouds, where they drop silver iodide flares on them. The chemical particles act like a scaffold for water molecules to crystallize on, causing snow to form and fall before the water molecules turn into hail.

COLD AS ICE

Giant hailstones are scary but not as terrifying as the 20-foot piece of ice that fell from the sky in Ross-shire, Scotland, in 1849. Recorded in the *Guinness World Records*, the shard appeared to be composed of smaller pieces—possibly multiple hailstones that fused together after being struck by lightning.

6 WHAT HAPPENED TO THE HOLE IN OUR OZONE LAYER?

Back in the 1980s, when hair spray, giant car phones, and ridiculous shoulder pads were transforming life as we knew it, something else was impacting our planet on a catastrophic scale . . .

IN THE OZONE

Ozone is a gas containing three oxygen atoms in its molecule, unlike regular oxygen that just has two. Its name comes from the Greek *ozein*, meaning "to smell," because of the gas's stinky odor. As far back as the 19th century, scientists had figured out that ozone was a key component of Earth's atmosphere. Then, in 1913, French scientists Charles Fabry and Henri Buisson took measurements that determined a layer of ozone was present in our planet's stratosphere—9.3 to18.6 miles above the surface.

They also proved that this "ozone layer" blocked out the sun's high-frequency ultraviolet rays, acting as an effective shield for life on Earth. As we now know, ultraviolet (UV) rays are extremely dangerous, causing skin cancer and other health problems for humans, as well as severely damaging other wildlife and organisms.

CFC YOU LATER

CFCs were making their way into the upper atmosphere, where the UV light breaks up the chemical's molecular bonds, freeing chlorine atoms into the air. The chlorine then bonds with oxygen atoms, stealing them from ozone molecules and causing the layer to be depleted.

The discovery caused a public panic as people worried about the effects of this giant "hole." Action was swift. In 1987, 24 nations signed the Montreal Protocol strictly limiting the use of CFCs. This agreement became the first United Nations (UN) treaty to be signed by every country in the UN.

HOLEY MOLEY!

In 1985, scientists working at the Halley Research Station in Antarctica discovered something they had long suspected: the ozone layer was thinning, reducing ozone levels above Antarctica by 65 percent. And what was the cause? Well, the 1980s craze for hairspray wasn't entirely blameless. Rather than emissions from supersonic aircraft or the space race, it was CFCs (chlorofluorocarbons), chemicals used in spray bottles for decades, that were the cause. This theory earned the scientists who discovered it the Nobel Prize in 1974, but the real damage researchers in Antarctica found a decade later was far worse than they predicted.

THE BIG SHRINK

Since the 1985 discovery, scientists have come to better understand the ozone layer and its "hole." Every spring when the weather warms up, the heat causes the reaction between CFCs and ozone to increase, but then over the winter the hole has time to recover. There have also been "holes" discovered over Tibet and the Arctic. Overall the Antarctic hole is getting smaller, in large part because of the Montreal Protocol. And scientists think that by 2080 the global ozone layer will have returned to the way it was in the 1950s.

O-NO?

There's no doubt the growth of CFCs was disastrous for the ozone layer and life on Earth, but there is some concern that its replenishment means an increase in global warming in the Antarctic region, since a thinner ozone layer helped to release trapped heat and create cooling clouds.

7 WHAT MAKES A SNOWSTORM A BLIZZARD?

Not all snowstorms can be classified as a blizzard. In order to earn the moniker, a snowstorm must meet three criteria: wind speed must be 30 knots (35 miles per hour) or more, visibility must be significantly reduced, and the storm must last for at least three hours.

BRING ON THE BLIZZARD

If these three conditions aren't met, then the storm is normally classified as a "winter storm" or "heavy snow." Although freezing temperatures often accompany blizzards, they're no longer a requirement for a storm to be considered one. In the past, blizzards were categorized by their temperature as well, with −20°F or lower being the benchmark. Other languages have different words to describe severe snowstorms. Some of the world's fiercest snowstorms occur in Russia, where they have several specific words for snowstorms, including these four: *metel* is used to describe wind-driven snow, *v'yuga* is a literary term for a snowstorm, and *buran* and *purga* describe region-specific blizzards.

The dreaded *purga* normally arrives in northern Siberia every winter. The storm travels from the north or northeast of the region and stampedes across the Kamchatka Peninsula. It's so strong and the air is filled with so much snow that people cannot open their eyes and struggle to breathe and stand upright. The extreme weather is disorienting to the point where people have been found frozen to death a short distance from their homes. The *buran* in southern Siberia is a different beast. While the temperatures are actually warmer, the snow-filled wind is so strong that it feels much colder. The Soviets named their first reusable spacecraft *Buran* after this impressive and powerful storm.

CHILLING HISTORY

Some of the worst blizzards on record have taken place in the United States. More than 400 people died during the Great Blizzard of 1888, when up to 50 inches of snow was dumped on Massachusetts, Connecticut, New Jersey, and New York. The coastal blizzard saw some 200 ships lost to the waves as well. The Super Bowl Blizzard of 1975 had a much lower human death toll of 58, but the heavy snowstorms in the Midwest took the lives of 100,000 farm animals that year. In more recent years, a 1993 blizzard received the title of "Storm of the Century" because of the dramatic impact felt across the northeastern United States and the loss of 300 lives. This region's blizzards are known as nor'easters.

DEADLIEST BLIZZARD

Due to dangerous driving conditions and freezing temperatures, blizzards pose a significant threat to human lives and are almost always deadly when they hit. The deadliest blizzard on record took place in Iran in 1972 and lasted for six days. Some villages were completely buried by the snow, and by the end of the ordeal an estimated 4,000 people had been killed.

8 WHY DOES RAIN SMELL SO GOOD?

There's nothing quite like the smell after it's rained—perfumes and air fresheners have tried to capture it, but there's no substitute for the real thing. That smell has a name, "petrichor," coined by two Australian scientists who in 1964 set out to determine the cause.

SMELLS LIKE RAIN

The scientists figured out that a main cause is a blend of oils secreted by some plants when the earth is dry. When it rains, these oils are released into the air and mix with other substances, producing that unmistakable aroma. One of these, called geosmin, is made by bacteria in the soil. When the rain lands on the ground, it forces bacteria spores into the air with the geosmin, creating that wondrous whiff.

ANTHROPOLOGICALLY SPEAKING...

The fact that rain smells so good to humans could also be a result of evolution. Some studies have shown that the human nose can identify even highly diluted geosmin. Scientists studying Australia's Pitjantjatjara people observed a clear association between the smell of rain and the color green. This sensory alliance illustrates a deep-rooted association in this often arid area between the season's first rain and the plant growth that usually follows it.

THUNDEROUS RECEPTION

There is sometimes a distinctive "chlorine" smell in the air before a thunderstorm, the result of lightning splitting oxygen and nitrogen molecules in the atmosphere. They then re-form as nitric oxide, which collides with other chemicals in the air to produce ozone. Ozone travels long distances, so you might indeed smell the storm coming.

9 CAN TWO SNOWFLAKES BE IDENTICAL?

When Wilson Bentley started photographing snowflakes in 1885 in Jericho, Vermont, the idea that no two snowflakes are alike was born. His photographs showed how, seen under a microscope, each snowflake's individual pattern was different. But that was over a century ago—surely someone's found a matching pair by now?

MORE THAN MEETS THE EYE

Snowflakes, or snow crystals as they are more accurately called, are created when cloud-based water vapor cools and, rather than becoming liquid, it crystallizes around microscopic dust particles. These crystals all start as small hexagonal plates, and the six "arms" are formed where more water molecules land. As the crystal falls to the ground, the humidity and temperature changes it encounters will inform its unique shape.

LOOK A LITTLE CLOSER

It's possible (but unlikely) that two snowflakes could experience the same conditions in nature, causing them to appear identical. However, on a molecular level they can never match completely. Water molecules are made up of two hydrogen atoms and an oxygen atom, but not all hydrogen atoms are the same. While most consist of a proton and an electron, a few hundred out of every million also contain a neutron. This hydrogen isotope is called deuterium. Millions of water molecules make up a snowflake, and one in 3,000 of these contain deuterium instead of hydrogen. The vast number of variable positions of these molecules within the snowflake's structure means no two snowflakes can be completely identical.

10 WHY ARE THERE NO TYPHOONS IN THE ATLANTIC?

A typhoon is a tropical storm with winds of 74 miles per hour or more. You won't find typhoons in the Atlantic, because when a tropical storm reaches that wind speed there, it's called a hurricane. The word "typhoon" refers to extreme tropical storms in the western North Pacific.

THE EYE OF THE STORM

Typhoons and hurricanes are both severe tropical cyclones—the generic term for a rotating storm system that starts out at sea. At the center of any cyclone is the eye—the area around which the storm is rotating. This can be anywhere between 12 and 30 miles in diameter. Underneath the eye, the sky above is often clear and the winds are less strong—it's usually the calmest point, the result of the strong winds converging around the eye wall but never reaching the eye itself.

IT CAME FROM THE SEA...

The year 1780 was a particularly bad one for hurricanes in the Caribbean, but none were more catastrophic than the Great Hurricane of October 10 and 11, one of the deadliest tropical storms of all time. It claimed the lives of an estimated 22,000 people, not to mention the thousands who died as a result of the famine left in its

STORM BABIES

A study published in 2010 in the *Journal of Population Economics* studied fertility data in relation to tropical storms affecting the Atlantic and Gulf Coast of the United States, to determine any correlation between people hunkering down for a storm and the number of babies that resulted. It found that when a "watch" was issued, meaning a tropical storm could hit within 36 hours, there was a 2 percent surge in births nine months later. But when a more imminent "warning" was issued, giving 24 hours' notice, the opposite effect occurred—up to a 2 percent decrease.

wake. There was little to alert people to an impending hurricane, so Barbados's residents would have had no warning when the storm struck—flattening houses, capsizing ships, and destroying sugarcane fields. Barbados wasn't the only island to face the storm's wrath—most of the eastern Caribbean was left in ruins.

WHAT'S IN A NAME?

While working in Australia, the 19th-century British meteorologist Clement Wragge devised a system using Greek letters and then mythological character names to keep track of local storms. When those ran out, Wragge named the worst storms after politicians to whom he'd taken a disliking.

During World War II, U.S. meteorologists began naming Pacific storms after their wives and girlfriends. In the 1950s, a two-year period saw U.S. storms officially named using the phonetic alphabet, a system abandoned in favor of women's names in 1953. This stuck, despite feminist protests, until 1978 for eastern North Pacific storms and 1979 for Atlantic storms, when men's names were added to the rotating roster. Now six lists of 26 names (one for each letter in the alphabet) are recycled every six years. Names are usually retired and replaced if a storm causes significant damage or loss of life.

11 WHAT DO THE SWISS HAVE AGAINST SNOWMEN?

The Swiss are a notoriously peaceful people—but not on the third Monday in April every year. That's the day crowds gather to see a snowman made from cotton paraded through Zurich. But don't be fooled by this charming pageantry—that snowman's life soon comes to a rather explosive end.

THE END OF WINTER

Dating back to the 19th century, to mark the end of winter the Swiss celebrate Sechseläuten, which translates to "ringing of the six o'clock bell." Part of the festivities involves the parade of a 10-foot-tall fabric Frosty, known as a Böögg, which is stuffed full of dynamite. After making his way through town, he's placed on a bonfire.

When the bells of Zurich's Grossmünster cathedral chime six o'clock in the evening, the bonfire is lit, and soon after the snowman explodes. It's thought that the longer it takes for the Böögg to blow up, the longer it will be till spring arrives. The festival has taken place in this form annually since 1904, except for the World War II years when all green spaces were used to plant potatoes and there was nowhere to have the bonfire.

QUICK FACT

ARTISTIC SNOWMEN
Snowmen have been around since at least the Middle Ages and were often created by famous artists for the nobility. When Michelangelo was only 19, he was commissioned by the ruler of Florence to make one for his mansion's courtyard.

QUIZ
WEATHER AND CLIMATE

Test how much you've learned about the world's weird weather with this quick quiz.

QUESTIONS:

1. "Identical twin" snowflakes are identical on a molecular level—true or false?

2. How is the Swiss exploding Böögg snowman similar to Groundhog Day?

3. Is the "Cappuccino Coast" found in California or Australia?

4. What is the name of the sound crickets make with their legs?

5. Name one other word for blizzard.

6. Petrichor is a distinctive smell created by a blend of oils that are released when it rains—true or false?

7. Do sand dunes move faster or slower if there is lots of vegetation in their path?

8. The hole in the ozone is now shrinking. True or false?

9. Which country has recorded the heaviest hailstone in the world?

10. Typhoons occur in the Pacific, but what do they call extreme tropical cyclones that happen in the Atlantic?

Turn to page 244 for the answers.

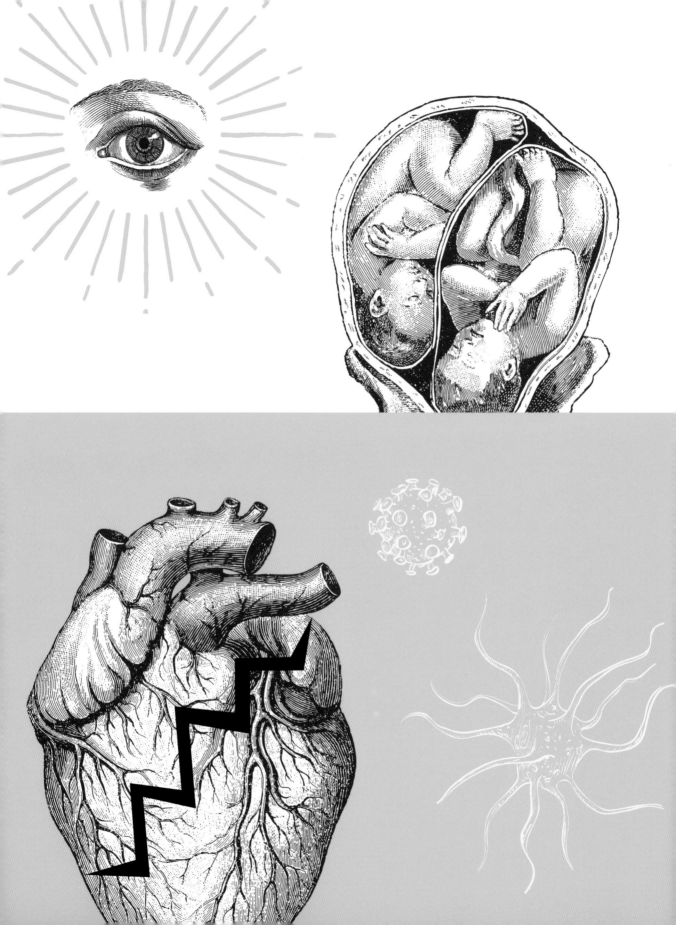

THE HUMAN BODY

12 WHICH BONE IS MAKING A COMEBACK?

There's no doubt the human body has evolved over time, but when it comes to one little bone scientists thought was heading to the vaults of history, the future's looking bright.

BEAN AND GONE

The fabella, meaning "little bean," is a sesamoid bone behind the kneecap. Most sesamoids are pretty small, and their job is to help distribute pressure evenly as we walk. Some people can have up to 20, while some people don't have any at all. The fabella, which people can live quite happily without and have been doing so for generations, still appears randomly in some knees. Analysis of medical literature on the legs dating back over 150 years showed that in 1918 only about 11 percent of the world population had them. But research carried out by Imperial College London in 2018 found that the bone's been on the rise, and is now present in 39 percent of humans.

MAKE NO BONES ABOUT IT

Researchers don't really know what the bone's original purpose was and why only some people have it. Similarly to other sesamoids, it might help reduce friction, redirect muscle forces when we move, or help increase the knee's muscle power. One reason posed for its gradual return is that our diets are making humans taller and heavier, putting our knees under more pressure, and the bones have grown in response. Unfortunately, rather than providing superhero-like powers, fabellae might actually be causing problems. Osteoarthritic knee patients are twice as likely to have them, and some people experience pain caused directly by their fabellae.

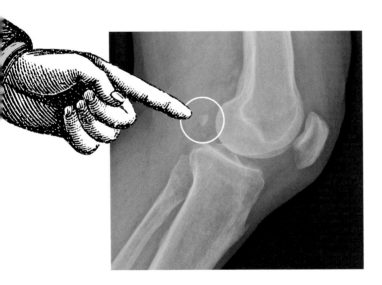

13 CAN YOU MOVE AFTER DEATH?

No one's suggesting that zombies are leaping from the grave on the hunt for human brains, but when we're laid to rest after we die, we don't stay as still as you'd think . . .

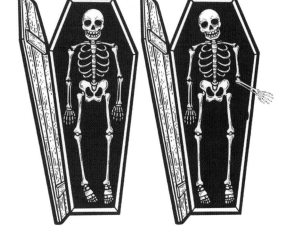

NOT SO STILL AS THE GRAVE

The stiffening and then relaxing effects of rigor mortis, bloating from intestinal gases, and the small movements caused by larvae hatched in the body have been quite well documented, but research carried out at the Australian Facility for Taphonomic Experimental Research by Central Queensland University discovered that our bodies can move for up to a year after we have died. They were investigating how bodies decompose, or not, under different conditions. Without the interference of wildlife to contend with, over 17 months they filmed and studied one corpse. Surprisingly, they noticed significant movements caused by the body itself. For example, the arms were initially placed alongside the body, but at one point they shifted and were flung to the side. The likely causes were thought to be mummification and the ligaments drying out.

CRACKING THE CASE

Developing a greater understanding of what happens to our bodies after we die can be very useful for crime scene investigators, especially when a body is discovered a significant time after death. Knowing when these physical shifts occur can provide forensic scientists with much more accurate estimates when determining time of death, and can help investigators avoid inaccurate deductions about a crime scene because of the position of a victim's body.

14 WHY ARE SOME PEOPLE LEFT-HANDED?

Lefties are a rare breed—making up a consistent 10 to 15 percent of the global population. But why do people have a dominant hand at all, and what causes it to be your left rather than your right?

MONKEYING AROUND

Humans aren't the only creatures to have a preferred hand for performing specific tasks. Chimpanzees use one hand over the other to become adept at performing certain tasks that require dexterity, such as termite fishing. Using a stick, chimps poke around in a termite mound, determining the size of the hole and how full of termites it might be. They build up the skill in their chosen hand to slowly pull the stick out before gobbling up the unsuspecting termites. However, unlike humans, there's a 50/50 split between right-handed and left-handed chimps. So where does our right bias come from?

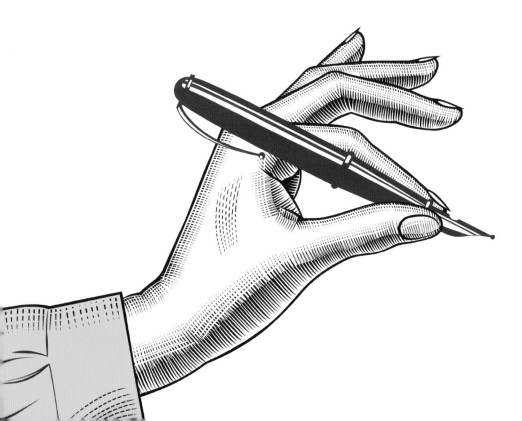

THEORY IN HAND

Unlike other, less common genetic traits in humans, which have been determined to be recessive—meaning over time they would be forced out of the genetic pool—left-handedness persists. It's thought that a number of different genes might be responsible for the outcome, and that they're the genes that relate to the development of your body's asymmetry.

One theory proposes that two different gene variants at the same genetic location are in part responsible for our handedness. One is the most common, and promotes right-handedness, while the other is less common, but if it is in your genetic heritage, there's a 50 percent chance you will be left-handed.

RIGHT TO NURTURE

We also know that for those individuals for whom left-handedness might be a genetic option based on the theory above, external cultural and societal pressures can also play a big part in influencing handedness. It also explains why a left-handed child can be born to two right-handed parents or vice versa. Unfortunately, history has shown itself to be suspicious of left-handedness— the Catholic Church oppressed lefties in the Middle Ages in Europe, associating them with the devil, and later writing with your left hand was considered evidence of witchcraft. Rigid education systems of the 18th, 19th, and even 20th centuries did little to correct these assumptions that left equaled bad and right equaled good.

SUCK IT AND SEE

Handedness starts in the womb, determined before we ever get our hands on a crayon. A study conducted at Queen's University, Belfast, studied ultrasounds of fetuses inside the womb and found that nine out of ten sucked their right thumb rather than their left. The right-thumb-suckers went on to become right-handed children and those who chose their left thumb became left-handed.

TO THE LEFT, TO THE LEFT

Did you know that handedness isn't the only way your body picks a preference for left or right? We all have a dominant ear, eye, and even foot. In contrast to left-handedness, more of us—roughly 40 percent—are left-eared, 30 percent are left-eyed, and 20 percent are left-footed.

15 WHAT DOES YOUR EYE COLOR SAY ABOUT YOU?

They say the eyes are the window to the soul, and while it's a bit of a stretch to read minds by staring at someone intently, there are some revealing things to be learned from looking someone in the eye, including their ancestry, health, pain threshold, and alcohol tolerance.

IN YOUR GENES

Scientists used to think that one gene determined eye color. They now know that there are multiple genes, as many as 13, that determine your eye color. Two genes in particular—known as OCA2 and HERC2—are responsible for eye color, and you get one copy of each from each parent. These, combined with other color-affecting genes, result in a veritable rainbow of possibilities. The genes determine how much of the pigment melanin is produced by the melanocyte stroma cells in your iris. The more melanin that's produced, the more brown your eyes will be. Scientists believe that up until about 6,000 to 10,000 years ago, all humans would have had brown eyes, but a genetic mutation created a switch, preventing the production of melanin and causing the first blue-eyed humans. Potentially, all blue-eyed people are descendants of a common ancestor.

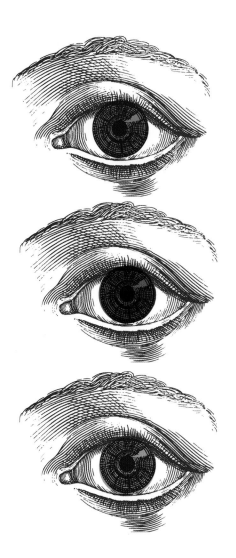

PAIN AND PUNCH

A study that investigated how women with different-colored eyes experienced pain during childbirth indicated that those with darker-colored eyes felt more physical pain and had more anxiety and depressive thoughts. On the positive side for those women, another study showed that their lighter-eyed counterparts could handle larger quantities of alcohol and were therefore more likely to abuse it.

BABY BLUES

When babies are born, they have less melanin in their eyes, so the color is often blue, and then by the age of three their true eye color is known. While some babies of African or Asian descent are born with blue eyes, most are born with brown eyes due to the higher level of melanin in their eyes at birth. The biggest variety of eye color can be seen in European populations, where brown is the most common, followed by blue or gray. Green is the rarest.

HEALTH ALERT

Eye color has been researched in relation to specific health conditions, including vitiligo. American researchers who studied a sample of 3,000 sufferers of the skin condition found that it was significantly less common in blue-eyed people with European ancestry compared to those with tan or brown eyes. Lighter-color eyes are more sensitive to UV rays, and are therefore at increased risk of melanoma of the uvea.

16 IS THE COMMON COLD REALLY THAT COMMON?

The "common cold" describes more than 200 viruses that cause a mild infection of the nose, throat, and airways. Of these, about half are the more common human rhinoviruses (HRV), the cause of around 40 percent of colds. So, some "common colds" are more common than others.

QUICK FACT

THE COST OF A COLD

Colds are big business, with the U.S. market spending up to $5 billion per year on over-the-counter treatments. But the cost to big business is even more. With nearly 110 million lost days of work and school combined in the United States alone, it's been calculated that $25 billion is lost in productivity every year.

COMMONLY SPEAKING

Because there are over 100 known variants of HRV alone, it's impossible to create a cold vaccine. As a result, this frequently received infectious disease has earned its name—most adults will get two to four different colds per year, and children even more. However, once you've had a cold, your body develops antibodies to that strain of the virus—so the more colds you've had, the less likely it is that you will catch a cold in the future.

People over the age of 50 are 50 percent less susceptible to catching colds than teenagers, and researchers have also found that those who have a healthier lifestyle, more sleep, and lower stress levels suffer less from colds than others. And a study has shown that those blessed with longer telomeres (the little "caps" on your white blood cells that protect chromosomes from damage) are less likely to catch the common cold.

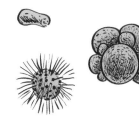

17 CAN YOU DIE FROM A BROKEN HEART?

Stress-induced cardiomyopathy—also known as broken heart syndrome—can affect a person with an otherwise healthy heart. Women are more likely to experience the intense chest pain, often misdiagnosed as a heart attack, caused by the surge of stress hormones released during an emotionally stressful event.

DEATH BY HEARTACHE

Another name for the condition is takotsubo cardiomyopathy. *Takotsubo* is a Japanese word for a type of round-bottomed, narrow-necked vessel—the shape of your heart's left ventricle when you're suffering from the syndrome. The left ventricle enlarges and the heart doesn't pump well, leading to an abnormal heartbeat, which, if left untreated, can result in a cardiac arrest. Other symptoms include breathlessness and intense chest pain. There is no specific treatment for takotsubo cardiomyopathy, but a patient may be prescribed medication to ease the symptoms. So, while it is possible that a broken heart could result in death, most people make a full recovery within a few weeks.

LOVE YOU TO DEATH

Three-quarters of those diagnosed with stress-induced cardiomyopathy have recently experienced significant emotional or physical stress—a bereavement, a traumatic breakup, or even a happy shock, like winning the lottery. But it is sometimes cited as the reason for elderly partners dying within a short period of each other. Research has shown that there is an increased risk of death after the hospitalization of a partner, but after six months that increase is diminished.

18 IS CHOCOLATE THE CURE FOR ALL ILLS?

In North America and Europe, people eat a lot of chocolate. While we've come to view that sweet brown candy as a contributor to our expanding waistlines, some scientists are actively encouraging people to indulge their inner chocolate addict—in moderation.

ONLY THE BEST

But it's not just any chocolate that will suffice. Cacao beans, from which cocoa is derived, contain antioxidants that boost your immune system. They're packed with more nutrients than some so-called super fruits, like acai berries. Natural cocoa powder and dark chocolate are good sources. Unlike its milkier cousin, which contains milk and cream, a small amount of dark chocolate with at least 65 percent cacao might do you a world of good.

TREAT THAT TICKLY COUGH

A 2012 study by the British National Health Service found that persistent coughs were dramatically improved in 60 percent of patients after they were given a course of theobromine—a chemical derived from cacao beans. Another study showed that the chemical can block the action of the sensory nerves, preventing the cough reflex.

BE SERIOUS

But it's not just a tickly cough that dark chocolate has been shown to help. Here are a few other suspected cacao cures:

• DEMENTIA
Harvard University researchers found that two cups of hot chocolate every day could improve mental performance in the elderly. They measured blood flow to the brain—normal levels of which are essential for cognition. In one group, which had impaired blood flow, they noticed an 8 percent increase after a month.

• CANCER
While eating chocolate on a regular basis has not been found to prevent cancer, one study showed that pentamer, which is found in chocolate, deactivates proteins that cause cancer cells to divide.

• DIABETES
Surely diabetics should be steering clear of chocolate? Well, apparently not, according to an Italian study that found the flavonoids in dark chocolate could be used to lower blood pressure and increase metabolism of sugar—a protective measure for diabetics.

A CURE THROUGH THE AGES

Contemporary scientists are not the first to study the benefits of chocolate. While chocolate's modern history began in the 1500s with the Spanish exploration of South America, cacao beans were a necessary part of ancient civilizations—used for trade and offered up to deities. *The Florentine Codex*, a 1590 document created by a Spanish priest who lived in what is now Mexico, lists several medicinal uses for chocolate, including improvements in asthma, angina, and cancer, as well as increased energy and decreased agitation.

HOW MUCH DO WE EAT?

In the United States alone, each person consumes around 10 pounds of chocolate every year. But 16 of the top 20 chocolate-eating countries are European. In 2015, a *Forbes* survey found that the Swiss eat the most per capita—19.8 pounds, to be exact.

19 CAN TWINS COMMUNICATE TELEPATHICALLY?

With their uncanny physical similarities and matching DNA and blood type, twins—especially identical twins—have always fascinated researchers. The study of twins—gemellology—has produced several remarkable results over the years. Yet despite overwhelming anecdotal evidence, no scientific study has found proof of extrasensory perception (ESP) between twins.

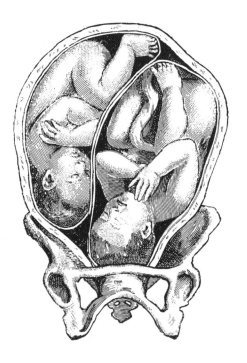

EMOTIONALLY ATTUNED

Twins often make tabloid headlines when one experiences stomach pains as the other is going into labor, or when they are raised apart but end up married to partners with the same name. If they're not reading each other's minds, how are some of these occurrences possible? Some believe the amount of time twins spend together in the womb and in childhood makes them especially attuned to each other's emotions. A 1993 British study of the levels of ESP and thought concordance—the ability to think like each other—in twins, compared to other siblings, found that twins had a marginally higher thought concordance level. But when it came to ESP, there was no evidence that twins had some otherworldly connection. Apparently, they just make better news stories.

A SECRET LANGUAGE

Twins' similar speech patterns and life experiences mean they often finish each other's sentences or each seem to know what the other is going to say next. Telepathy might be unproven in twins, but that doesn't mean they don't have their own special way of communicating. About 40 percent of twins invent their own "language" in childhood. This phenomenon is called *cryptophasia*, derived from the Greek for "secret speech." Most children develop some of their own words or codes with their siblings, but because of twins' synched-up development, they often come up with a version of their mother tongue with which they can communicate easily. Arguably, most of these "languages" are not different languages at all but mispronunciations of their mother tongue that both twins are able to understand— an in-joke. Some twins have created more developed languages of their own, which scientists say tend to follow the same simple structure, no matter where the twins are from or what their native language is.

THE KENNEDY SISTERS

Most twins grow out of using their own language as they learn to speak to their parents and play with other children. In some cases, however, where twins are isolated and receive little outside influence, they have been known to continue their twin-speak into late childhood. Perhaps the most famous case of this was that of the Kennedy sisters. Growing up in 1970s San Diego, Grace and Virginia Kennedy were splashed across the newspapers when it was revealed that, at the age of six, they didn't speak any English, only their own secret language. Childhood convulsions had led their parents to believe they had a mental disability.

They were largely confined to the house and looked after by their German grandmother. Their language, it turned out, was a mixture of badly pronounced German and English. After undergoing speech therapy, both girls could speak English, but their language capabilities always lagged behind their peers.

20 HOW LONG AGO DID COSMETIC SURGERY BEGIN?

Transforming the human body through surgery for aesthetic reasons is nothing new. While surgical procedures today are far more advanced, healers, doctors, and even barbers have been performing cosmetic procedures for centuries.

ANCIENT HEALERS

Plastic surgery gets its name from the Greek word for these types of procedures: *plastikos*, meaning "molding." It's believed early Indian communities widely experimented with shaping parts of the body, particularly the nose, for aesthetic effect. One of the first people to record these cosmetic procedures was an Indian healer known as Sushruta. Scholars believe he lived at some point between 1000 and 600 BC, and today we know much of his medicine from *Sushruta Samhita,* a 184-page compendium of his teachings. Among these writings, Sushruta described reconstructive methods for different defects, including rhinoplasty—or nose jobs—using a pedicled forehead flap. After this was published in the *Gentleman's Magazine of Calcutta* in 1794, it began to be used more widely in Europe. This technique is still known today as the Indian flap.

NECRO NIP AND TUCK

Egyptians avoided surgical procedures in life as they believed you should remain as nature intended. They did, however, make some modifications to corpses to emphasize prominent features in order to highlight the person's identifying feature in the afterlife. Ramses II's corpse had a small bone and a handful of seeds inserted into his nose, and bandages were inserted into the cheeks and bellies of other mummies.

NO EASY JOB

Fifteenth-century rhinoplasties, performed long before the advent of anesthesia and hygienic hospital practices, were described by Heinrich von Pfolspeundt in his 1460 work *Buch der Bundth-Ertznei.* A flap of skin, roughly shaped like a nose flattened out, was cut out of the patient's arm, leaving the bottom of the new nose flap attached. The patient's raised arm would be bound to their head, with the nose flap positioned in place. The patient would then spend up to ten days with their arm attached to their nose before the skin flap was cut.

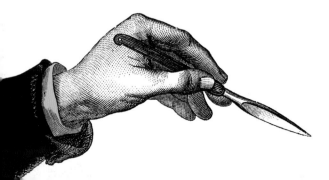

FIVE QUICK FACTS

1 YOUR SALIVA IS UNSTOPPABLE

We recycle saliva with the flow rate of around 0.1 fluid ounce per hour. That works out to a wine bottle per day, or around 20,000 liters in your lifetime.

2 SIZE MATTERS MOST IN THE MORNING

If you have a height complex, measure yourself first thing in the morning, when you'll be about a centimeter taller. During the day the cartilage between your bones gets squished and you lose that vital centimeter.

3 NOT ALL OF OUR BODY NEEDS BLOOD TO SURVIVE

The cornea is the only body part where the cells aren't served by blood vessels. Instead, they get all the oxygen and nutrients they need from tear fluid, aqueous humor, and nerve fibers.

4 EVERYBODY FARTS

People fart on average 10–20 times per day and produce around 16–50 fluid ounces of gas—that's enough to fill a party balloon.

5 SOME TUMORS ARE TERA-FYING

Tumors are scary at the best of times, but some people develop teratomas—from the Greek meaning "monster swelling"—that grow their own teeth and hair.

21 CAN YOUR STOMACH BE EMBARRASSED?

When we blush from embarrassment, it's a result of our body releasing adrenaline as part of the fight-or-flight response. Your heart rate speeds up, and so does your breathing, as you prepare to run from the awkward situation you've just gotten into. But it's not just your face that turns bright red.

BLUSHING INSIDE AND OUT

You might not notice, but there's lots happening on the inside too: your digestive system slows down to redirect energy to your muscles, your pupils dilate to help you take in your surroundings, and your blood vessels also expand so that blood can move oxygen around your body more easily.

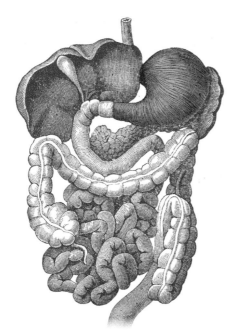

When the veins in your face dilate, more blood flows through them than normal, causing the reddened cheeks we associate with public humiliation. But as your stomach is lined with blood vessels, they are also expanding, blushing in solidarity with your face, even if no one can see.

SOCIAL EXPECTATIONS

Science has struggled to answer the question: why do we blush when we're embarrassed? Many believe blushing evolved as a way of enforcing social codes. When we blush, others can visibly see we know that what we've said or done might not be seen as acceptable. In a sense, it's a nonverbal apology. This adrenaline-based blushing, which is different from blushing caused by heat, alcohol consumption, or arousal, is something that develops in children when they start to become socially aware and conscious of others' feelings, supporting the theory that it developed as a societal function.

22 WHY ARE BARBERSHOP POLES RED AND WHITE?

In many countries, especially in the West, men know where they can go for a short back and sides, a shave, and some manly bonding by the red-and-white barber's pole. Its origins lie in the bloodletting practices of medieval barbershops, where getting a cut meant something entirely different.

A BLOODY AFFAIR

Bloodletting was a typical treatment for a whole host of conditions in the Middle Ages. From gout and epilepsy to smallpox and even the plague, ordinary people would visit their barber for this treatment, after priests were banned by the Catholic Church from administering the procedure. A special tool that included a blade, known as a fleam, was used to nick veins or arteries in the arm or neck, and blood would flow into a small brass bowl or wooden cup. Sometimes leeches were used to let blood instead. In England in 1540, barbers and surgeons became one profession under King Henry VIII, and these "barber-surgeons" could perform enemas, sell medicine, extract teeth, and, of course, cut hair.

POLES, NOT BOWLS

To advertise their services, barbers would put the brass bowls of their clients' blood in the window. In 1307 a law was passed that forbade this vulgar display, and the barber pole emerged in its place. For the largely illiterate populace, the pole—signifying the red blood and white bandages involved in the practice—was a recognizable symbol of the surgical services the barber offered.

23 IS IT POSSIBLE TO SURVIVE RABIES?

In 2015, the World Health Organization (WHO) launched a global framework to eliminate human rabies deaths by 2030. The infectious viral disease is present on all continents except for Antarctica, but more than 95 percent of the tens of thousands of human deaths each year occur in Africa and Asia.

SHOCKING SYMPTOMS

Dog bites are the biggest cause of human rabies deaths, accounting for up to 99 percent of transmissions, although bats, raccoons, foxes, and cats, among others, can also be culprits. Infected animals pass on the disease through their saliva, either by biting, scratching, or a lick to broken skin, the mouth, or the eye. After a period of between a few days and three months, symptoms start to show, including fever and a tingling or burning sensation at the wound site. Then the disease manifests itself in one of two ways. "Furious rabies"

is more common, and the type most people think of when they imagine the disease. Symptoms include hyperactivity, excited behavior, hallucinations, and a fear of water. Once a person exhibits symptoms, death from drowning in their own spit or blood, inability to breathe, or cardiac arrest usually occurs within a couple of days. The other type, "paralytic rabies," sees the muscles gradually become paralyzed until death occurs.

RACE AGAINST THE CLOCK

Rabies is vaccine-preventable, although the vaccination is costly, meaning it's largely a disease suffered by poor and vulnerable populations. When a person has been bitten, it's a race against the clock to prevent the disease from entering the central nervous system, even if they've had the vaccine. If the wound is cleaned and the patient is given a potent course of the rabies vaccine, coupled with rabies antibodies if they've not had the vaccine pre-exposure, there is a good chance of survival. Every year, 15 million people receive a post-bite vaccination, which is thought to prevent hundreds of thousands of deaths. But for those who are unable to afford the treatment or don't realize they are infected, the disease is almost always fatal.

THE MILWAUKEE PROTOCOL

In 2004, a 15-year-old girl from Milwaukee, Wisconsin, was bitten by a rabid bat, and although her parents cleaned up the wound, they didn't seek medical treatment. Three weeks later the girl began to show symptoms of the disease. As it was too late to administer the vaccine or antibodies, doctors at the Children's Hospital of Wisconsin induced a coma, hoping the girl's immune system would build up antibodies to fight the virus, and it worked—she survived. However, in 2014 health officials labeled the "Milwaukee Protocol" a red herring after it failed to save 26 other patients. They believe the rabies strain that infected the girl might have been a milder, less virulent variant.

ORIGINS OF A NAME

The name "rabies" was coined in the 1590s from the Latin word *rabere*, meaning "to rage." The Greek philosopher Aristotle wrote of this ancient disease: "Dogs suffer from the madness. This causes them to become irritable and all animals they bite to become diseased."

24 ARE HATS BAD FOR YOUR HEALTH?

They're not anymore, but in the 18th and 19th centuries, when headwear was *de rigueur*, makers of felt hats were exposed to large quantities of mercury nitrate. Used in a process called carroting, this substance had a definite impact on people's health.

A POISONOUS PLACE TO WORK

Both for fashion and function, animal furs were a key material in hat production. Mercury nitrate caused the fur to turn orange, shrink, and become easier to remove from the skin, to be made into felt. Repeated exposure saw many workers develop symptoms of mercury poisoning, including emotional instability, memory loss, tremors, speech problems, and hallucinations. The British idiom "mad as a hatter" derives from this unfortunate side effect of working in the millinery industry.

UREA NEED TO USE THE WASHROOM

Originally, hatters used camel urine to strip the fur from animal skins. The urea component contains nitrogen, which helps to break down the proteins in the fur. Hatters would sometimes replace camel urine with their own, until it was noted that one workman's urine was producing better-quality felt. He was being treated for syphilis with mercury—thus the discovery that mercury nitrate worked wonders on fur.

THE MAD HATTER

One man thought to have suffered particularly from mad hatter syndrome is Boston Corbett—the hat worker turned Unionist who shot President Abraham Lincoln's assassin, John Wilkes Booth. He'd castrated himself seven years earlier with a pair of scissors to curb his libido, and ended up in a mental asylum in his 50s before escaping, never to be seen again.

QUIZ
THE HUMAN BODY

Is your brain bursting with human body trivia? Try this quiz to see how much you learned.

QUESTIONS:

1. Does fabella mean "little onion" or "little bean"?

2. What disease that's most commonly transmitted by a dog bite is named after the Latin *rabere*, meaning "to rage"?

3. Name an ailment or disease that chocolate has been shown to improve.

4. Cryptophasia is something 40 percent of twins experience. Is it their own way of walking or talking?

5. What camel-derived liquid did hat workers use to strip the furs of animal skins: saliva, urine, or blood?

6. Humans aren't the only species to have left- or right-handedness. True or false?

7. Blue is the rarest eye color. True or false?

8. Teenagers are more likely to catch a cold than those over 50 years old. True or false?

9. What colors are most barbershop poles?

10. When was the earliest cosmetic surgery recorded? Was it in the period between 1000 and 600 BC, or in the 15th century?

Turn to page 244 for the answers.

ART AND ARCHITECTURE

25 WHAT HAPPENED TO *MONA LISA'S* EYEBROWS?

While it's the enigmatic smile of Leonardo da Vinci's most well-known subject that's often debated, closer examination of her brow line throws up some interesting discoveries. *Mona Lisa*'s lack of eyebrows and lashes might be true to the fashion of the era, but more recent investigation has revealed she wasn't always brow-less.

HIGH-RESOLUTION REVELATION

In 2007, a French engineer spent 3,000 hours studying 240-megapixel scans of the early 16th-century portrait. Pascal Cotte was able to detect traces of a left eyebrow, invisible to the naked eye, which he believes has gradually eroded due to restoration and cleaning. This would marry with art historian Giorgio Vasari's 1550 description of the painting, in which he wrote:

"The eyebrows, through his having shown the manner in which the hairs spring from the flesh could not be more natural."

THE LAYERS BENEATH

Paintings like the *Mona Lisa*, and the linen canvas or wood they're usually painted on, are susceptible to environmental conditions—humidity, temperature, exposure to direct sunlight—and over time their appearance can change significantly. Old varnish on the original painting, or additional layers applied to help preserve it, yellows and darkens over time, obscuring the light and colors beneath. Art conservationists use techniques such as thinning the varnish and dry-cleaning using soft brushes, and rather than water. Saliva is sometimes used as a cleaning agent—the warmth and enzyme content act on the lipids and proteins found in dirt.

26 WHY ARE THE TAJ MAHAL'S TOWERS TILTED?

In 2004, the Archaeological Survey of India (ASI) dismissed claims that the Taj Mahal's minarets are in danger of collapsing, despite the fact that three of the four towers are tilted by 1.5–3 inches, and the fourth by 8.5 inches.

TOO HEAVY TO HANDLE

The "tilt" measurements were taken in 1941, when the monument received its first scientific survey, and according to the ASI, which surveys the structure every four years, no structural damage has been found in the more than 70 years since. It's possible that the Taj Mahal's chief architect, Ustad Ahmad Lahauri, designed the towers so they would deliberately lean away from the central crypt, where Mumtaz Mahal's casket would reside. Construction began in 1632 and continued for just over two decades—it wasn't uncommon in the 17th century for these architectural behemoths to collapse under their own weight or as the result of an earthquake, so perhaps Lahauri was just being cautious.

A LOVE TO LAST FOR CENTURIES

Mumtaz Mahal was the third wife of Indian emperor Shah Jahan and mother to 14 of his children. She passed away after complications from childbirth, and not long afterward her husband oversaw the construction of this lavish tomb—a final gift to his beloved. Around 20,000 people and 2,000 elephants worked to create the structure. When Shah Jahan died in 1666, he was also buried there. Other than the southwest tower's enthusiastic lean, his grave is the only component of the monument that is not completely symmetrical.

27 DID VAN GOGH CUT OFF HIS OWN EAR?

Self-Portrait with Bandaged Ear (1889) is one of Vincent van Gogh's most recognizable paintings. The bandaged right side of his face has fascinated art historians for decades—some believe he only sliced the earlobe, while others wonder if the wound was not self-inflicted at all.

AN EARFUL OF TRUTH

A letter found in an American archive, and penned by Van Gogh's doctor, Félix Rey, includes a diagram showing how the artist severed almost his entire ear, leaving a small part of the lobe intact. In 2009, a number of historians claimed that fellow painter and house guest Paul Gauguin had sliced off Van Gogh's earlobe in a sword fight. The injury described in Rey's notes, however, is consistent with the theory that a razor blade was used and that it was not an accident.

BANG

DOWNWARD SPIRAL

It is clear from his letters that Van Gogh suffered from bouts of depression, and it is thought that he cut off his ear after a dispute with Gauguin (the two men did not reconcile) or because he was unhappy that his brother was to be married. Either way, shortly after the incident Van Gogh was committed to the hospital for a time.

THE DEATH OF A PAINTER

Van Gogh died in 1890, the year after painting *Self-Portrait with Bandaged Ear*. In the mid-20th century, a small-caliber pocket revolver was found buried in the field outside Auvers, a suburb of Paris, where it is believed he shot himself in the chest. The corroded revolver, now owned by a private collector, goes some way toward explaining why the bullet that eventually killed him bounced off his rib—it took him some 30 hours to die from the wound. That type of gun, known as a *Lefaucheux à broche*, was more commonly used for scaring thieves than to kill.

In the years since his posthumous rise to fame, doctors have been diagnosing him with conditions such as bipolar disorder, lead poisoning, epilepsy, and thujone poisoning caused by the large quantities of absinthe he drank.

THE NOT-SO-LUCKY RECIPIENT

For many years it was widely believed that Van Gogh had gifted his severed ear to a sex worker named Rachel who resided in Arles, the French city that was Van Gogh's home for the last year of his life. But recent research has revealed that after the incident on December 23, 1888, Van Gogh made the aural offering to Gabrielle Berlatier, a young woman who worked as a maid at a brothel on Rue du Bout d'Arles. Not long before, she had been bitten by a rabid dog but survived after receiving a newly developed vaccine in Paris, where chemist Louis Pasteur had set up a special clinic to study and treat rabies. The cure was expensive, leaving her farming family in debt, which explains why she was working as a maid. She went on to marry and live to an old age, her encounter with the artist kept secret until long after her death.

28 CAN YOU REALLY SEE THE GREAT WALL OF CHINA FROM THE MOON?

The Great Wall is huge, stretching across northern China from Jiayuguan in the west to Shanhaiguan in the east. It is often hailed as the only man-made structure visible from the Moon. In fact, no man-made structures can be seen from the Moon. So why does it have this reputation?

THE HISTORY BOOKS

Nearly 200 years before humans set foot on the Moon, an English scholar proposed that the wall would be visible from space, while in 1895 journalist Henry Norman wrote: "The Great Wall of China is, after all, only a wall . . ." but that "besides its age

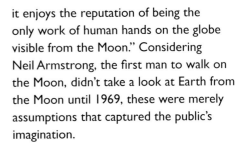

it enjoys the reputation of being the only work of human hands on the globe visible from the Moon." Considering Neil Armstrong, the first man to walk on the Moon, didn't take a look at Earth from the Moon until 1969, these were merely assumptions that captured the public's imagination.

When he returned to Earth, Armstrong was repeatedly asked what he could see from the Moon's surface, which is situated on average 230,000 miles from our planet. He said he could make out continents, lakes, and splotches of white on blue, but no man-made structures. This has been corroborated by other astronauts since. But still the belief in the wall's impressive scale persists, with many claiming that while it might not be visible from the Moon, it is visible from space.

A CHINESE MISSION

When Yang Liwei, China's first "taikonaut," returned from his first mission in 2003, he told reporters he had not seen the wall, much to the country's disappointment. (The term "taikonaut" is derived from the Chinese word *taikong*, meaning "space" or "cosmos," and the Greek word for sailor, *nautes*. It was coined by the English-language media to differentiate between American, Russian, and Chinese astronauts.) Other astronauts have claimed to have seen the wall from a low orbit when conditions are favorable, but that the wall's similar coloration to its surroundings makes it hard to spot with the naked eye. Moderate-resolution satellite images can sometimes spot the structure, but they are positioned a mere 440 miles above the Earth's surface. And with growing air pollution across China, the wall is becoming harder and harder to see from space.

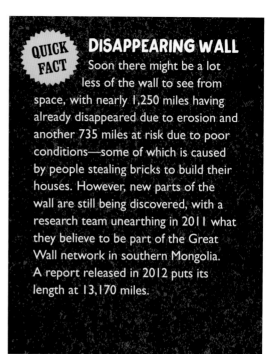

QUICK FACT

DISAPPEARING WALL

Soon there might be a lot less of the wall to see from space, with nearly 1,250 miles having already disappeared due to erosion and another 735 miles at risk due to poor conditions—some of which is caused by people stealing bricks to build their houses. However, new parts of the wall are still being discovered, with a research team unearthing in 2011 what they believe to be part of the Great Wall network in southern Mongolia. A report released in 2012 puts its length at 13,170 miles.

WHY CAN TOURISTS NO LONGER CLIMB THE STATUE OF LIBERTY'S TORCH?

At 305 feet 1 inch tall, and with a sway distance of 6 inches in 50-mile-per-hour winds, why would anyone want to climb Lady Liberty's torch? Nevertheless, before the Black Tom incident of 1916, it was possible for tourists to access the tip of the flame and savor the view.

IN THE DEAD OF NIGHT

On the night of July 30, 1916, guards alerted the Jersey City Fire Department when a fire broke out at the munitions depot on Black Tom Island, not far from Liberty Island. The guards were fleeing the scene when the firemen arrived, and with good reason: they knew that one barge was packed with 55 tons of TNT and 69 railcars were filled with thousands of tons of ammunition. These American-made weapons were waiting to be shipped to the Allied forces of World War I. When the fire reached the barge a little after 2:00 a.m., the series of explosions that followed would have measured 5.5 on the Richter scale. People felt the blast up to 90 miles away, including in Philadelphia, and many Manhattan and Jersey residents were thrown from their beds. The statue, including the torch, endured $100,000 worth of damage (equivalent to $2.34 million today) caused by debris from the explosions. Since then, the narrow, 40-foot-long ladder has been closed to the public.

CATCHING THE CULPRITS

The United States was not in World War I in 1916, but they were supplying the British and French with ammunition—much of which was being shipped from Black Tom Island. German spies had been fairly successful at destroying American ships and their cargo en route to assist the Allies. It was a Slovak immigrant named Michael

NEW TORCH, NEW TORCH

The Statue of Liberty is only a nickname—the real name is *Liberty Enlightening the World*. The torch is symbolic of enlightenment, while the seven spikes of the aureole are said to represent the world's seven continents. After the damage sustained to the raised arm and torch in 1916, and years of wear and tear, the original torch was replaced by a new one in 1986, made from copper and covered in 24-karat gold leaf. French sculptor Frédéric Bartholdi's original torch can be admired in the Pedestal Lobby at the base of the statue.

Kristoff, together with two Germans, who sabotaged the munitions depot that night. After the war, and once investigators had amassed enough evidence to bring about a claim, Germany was ordered to pay $50 million (equivalent to $1.17 billion today) to those who had suffered as a result of Black Tom—the single largest damage claim ever awarded by the Mixed Claims Commission.

CROWNING GLORY

While it's no longer possible for the public to climb to the dizzying heights of the torch, visitors to Liberty Island can still take in the sights of New York Harbor from the 25 windows of the statue's crown. The tourist attraction is not for the fainthearted, however, as you have to climb 377 steps to reach the viewing platform.

30 WHY DID MICHELANGELO MAKE ONE OF DAVID'S HANDS BIGGER THAN THE OTHER?

Heralded as one of the greatest sculptures in existence, Michelangelo's *David* is a masterpiece. But despite its exacting re-creation of the male form, the statue is out of proportion—the head and hands are unnaturally large. Art historians believe this is because of the work's planned location.

DAVID ON HIGH

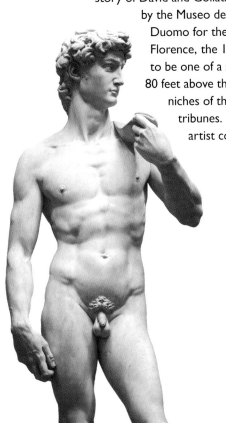

In 1501, Michelangelo began work on a marble sculpture of David from the biblical story of David and Goliath. Commissioned by the Museo dell'Opera del Duomo for the Cathedral of Florence, the 17-foot statue was to be one of a series to tower 80 feet above the ground in the niches of the cathedral's tribunes. It is thought the artist considered the

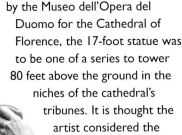

viewer's perspective, making the head and the hands, particularly the right, bigger to emphasize David's intentions as he prepares to fight Goliath. However, the finished statue was so good that it was displayed instead in the Piazza della Signoria, where a replica now stands. The real *David* was relocated to the Galleria dell'Accademia in 1873.

MARBLE MARVEL

Michelangelo was not the first to work on the block of marble. Almost 40 years previously, Agostino di Duccio had planned to sculpt a biblical prophet for the cathedral, but the project was abandoned. Ten years later another artist, Antonio Rossellino, took over the block, but deemed the marble to have too many imperfections, making it hard to work with. In 2005, scientists identified the origins of the marble—the Fantiscritti quarries in Miseglia—and confirmed its mediocre quality.

31 HOW CAN EGG WHITES HELP YOU CROSS A RIVER?

When a narrow wooden bridge was the only way to cross the Vltava River, the people of Prague wanted a sturdier solution, and they found it in the most unexpected place.

BRIDGE OF EGGS

It's hard to imagine building a colossal stone bridge, measuring 1,693 feet, without the engineering knowledge and technology we have today. Started in 1357, this sandstone marvel took over 50 years to build, but was constructed well enough to last to the present day. Known as the Charles Bridge after the king who got the project up and running, it could equally be called the "Egg Bridge," as legend had it that one of its key ingredients was egg whites. The mortar was strengthened by adding eggs, flour, and honey liqueur, and cities across Bohemia and Moravia sent eggs to help with the efforts. This was confirmed in 2008 when scientists at the Czech University of Chemical Technology found protein in the original mortar—they surmised that egg whites had indeed been used, mixed with milk or curd.

SPIRITUAL SCRAMBLE

Czechs weren't the only ones to make the most of the egg's binding properties. Millions of egg whites were used by Spanish colonialists in the Philippines to build impressive Catholic churches. They formed a mortar known as argamasa. Expense records for the construction of Manila Cathedral show duck eggs were a key ingredient and helped seal the structure with a layer of lime, powdered brick, and bamboo sap too.

32 WHY DIDN'T FRIDA KAHLO SMILE IN PHOTOGRAPHS?

Although considered one of Mexico's greatest modern artists, self-portrait painter Frida Kahlo's life was filled with hardship, tragedy, and disappointment, so she'd be easily forgiven for not grinning whenever someone whipped out a camera. However, that familiar stern expression has more to do with orthodontics than anything else—Frida Kahlo really didn't like her teeth.

PAIN AND POLIO

As an artist working to be appreciated in a male-dominated world, Kahlo's sans-smile persona (which shows in all of her self-portraits as well as photographs), coupled with her refusal to conform to gender norms, could have been a creative choice, but she also suffered more than most. She was diagnosed with polio at the age of six, which left her right leg noticeably thinner than her left. She was involved in a trolley accident, after which she faced a long road to recovery with a broken spine, pelvis, collarbone, and ribs. She suffered from multiple miscarriages and was later forced to terminate three pregnancies. This is thought to be due to the damage sustained to her uterus from the accident. She also suffered from an array of mental illnesses. She underwent 35 operations throughout her life, including the eventual amputation of her right leg below the knee.

TOLL ON HER TEETH

It's no surprise, then, that she had a bottle-a-day brandy habit, smoked like a chimney, and kept a constant supply of candy. All of which couldn't have done her teeth any favors. She was missing several teeth, including two incisors, which she replaced with two gold false ones. She also had a fancier pair of rose-gold choppers made for special occasions, studded with diamonds.

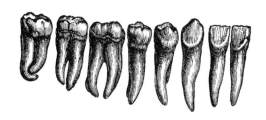

ANIMAL MAGIC

Surely if anything could make you crack a smile, it would be a menagerie of adorable creatures? While Kahlo managed to keep a serious expression, she probably had a whale of a time creating many of her self-portraits that feature animals—including her spider monkey, Fulang-Chang. She also had a trick-performing parrot, a fawn, an eagle, dogs, and a number of exotic birds that roamed around her garden.

DOCTOR KAHLO

If fate hadn't played its part, the world might never have seen the artworks of Frida Kahlo. She had planned to become a doctor, and in 1922 was one of a handful of women enrolled in the prestigious Escuela Nacional Preparatoria. It was after three years of study that she was seriously injured in the trolley car accident. To pass the three months she spent in a full-body cast, her father set up an easel over the bed, and she began to paint.

33 HAS ANYONE LIVED IN THE EIFFEL TOWER?

In 2016, a vacation rental company transformed a first-floor conference room in the Eiffel Tower into a luxury two-bedroom apartment, and four lucky contest winners got to call the tower home for a night. But there once was a man who could live there as he pleased.

HOME ON HIGH

Gustave Eiffel was an architect and civil engineer. He built the Eiffel Tower as part of the 1889 Exposition Universelle, which was taking place to celebrate the French Revolution's centennial. It took just over two years to build—an engineering feat of its time—and Eiffel made sure he would be able to enjoy the views better than anyone. On the third floor, at a height of just over 900 feet, three times the height of Notre Dame Cathedral, was a small apartment. Decorated with dark wood, patterned carpet, and wallpaper, and with all the trappings of a typical Parisian home (there was even a grand piano), this was a sanctuary in the sky for Eiffel to study and entertain.

THE PRICE OF PRIVACY

When word got out in Paris about Eiffel's apartment, he was besieged with requests to rent it. Everyone wanted a taste of tower living, but no price was high enough.

The lucky few who were invited to attend his private parties were the dignitaries and influential men of the day. Among them was Thomas Edison, the American inventor, who spent time smoking cigars and discussing his inventions with Eiffel. He even presented him with a gramophone. This scene is depicted with waxworks in the restored apartment space for today's visitors to view. And while you can't hang out with Eiffel himself, there is a champagne bar on the same level to raise a glass to him.

SCIENTIFIC STUDY

The tower was initially designed as a center for scientific research. In his initial proposal, Eiffel explained how the tower was perfectly suited to meteorological and astronomical observation. The apartment included a small laboratory for the engineer to explore his key areas of interest: wind, air resistance, and aviation. Eiffel spent the last 30 years of his life using the tower for practical applications, including wind resistance experiments and as a giant aerial for radio broadcasts.

FIVE QUICK FACTS

1 GUSTAV KLIMT REALLY LOVED CATS

The Austrian painter's studio was overrun with feline friends, and he even covered pages of his sketchbook in cat urine to act as a fixative.

2 VAN GOGH PAINTED AS A PATIENT

The Starry Night is one of the Dutch great's most famous works, but it was made while he was receiving treatment at a psychiatric hospital in Saint-Rémy, France. The hospital now has a wing named after him.

3 LEGO USED TO MAKE SPECIAL BRICKS FOR ARCHITECTS

The Modulex series was launched in 1963 with the aim of helping architects create models with the same stud-and-tube brick design of LEGO bricks. The only difference was that they were much smaller, measuring just half an inch long.

4 YVES KLEIN PAINTED WITH PEOPLE

Not content with regular paintbrushes, French artist Yves Klein turned female models into living brushes, painting them in his eponymous blue paint and having them lie or drag themselves across the canvas to create his Anthropometry series of works.

5 VIEWS ARE WORTH BIG MONEY

Tourists flocking to the Empire State Building's famous observation decks to see views of NYC earned the building's trust $111 million in 2014—$7 million more than leasing the building's office space.

34 WHY DID ANDY WARHOL PAINT CAMPBELL'S SOUP CANS?

Andy Warhol's iconic *Campbell's Soup Cans* (1962) has become symbolic of the 1960s pop art movement, and the man himself. Whether the painting is viewed as a comment on burgeoning American consumerism or mass manufacturing, one thing's for sure—Andy Warhol loved Campbell's Soup.

TWENTY YEARS OF SLURPING

Warhol famously said: "I used to drink it. I used to have the same lunch every day, for twenty years." He was talking, of course, about Campbell's Soup, the subject matter he chose to work with in 1962. He traced projections onto canvas and meticulously painted the outlines to reflect the lithograph printing style of the original labels.

While the 32 canvases might look identical at a glance, there is one for every flavor available that year, including Oyster Stew, Chicken 'N Dumplings, and Hot Dog Bean. Five of the paintings sold individually for $100, but the gallery owner bought them back when he realized the paintings made more sense as a group. He eventually sold them to New York's MoMA in 1996 for over $15 million.

THE SOUPER DRESS

This wasn't Warhol's only dalliance with the famous brand of soup; he produced a number of other works featuring the cans. He also printed his designs on paper dresses, which were worn by New York socialites. Wanting to cash in on their newfound cool appeal, in 1965 Campbell's Soup produced the Souper Dress—their own paper dress, which customers could buy for a dollar and two soup can labels.

QUIZ

ART AND ARCHITECTURE

Filled to the brim with artifacts and arty facts? Get to grips with what you've read with this little quiz.

QUESTIONS:

1. The Taj Mahal was a tomb for Emperor Shah Jahan's favorite elephant—true or false?

2. Which iconic tower was built for the 1889 Exposition Universelle in Paris?

3. What are the seven spikes on the Statue of Liberty's crown thought to represent: the seven continents or the seven deadly sins?

4. Saliva is sometimes used to restore oil paintings instead of water—true or false?

5. Which part of his body did Van Gogh famously cut off?

6. Why can't you see the Great Wall of China from the Moon?

7. What sort of eggs were used to help build Manila Cathedral?

8. What brand of soup did Andy Warhol famously paint—Heinz or Campbell's?

9. Michelangelo's *David* is based on David Schwimmer—true or false?

10. Which country was Frida Kahlo from: Canada, the United States, or Mexico?

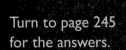

Turn to page 245 for the answers.

ANIMALS AND PLANTS

35 WHAT'S THE MOST PAINFUL INSECT STING?

Only three insects have had their sting rated "4" on the Schmidt Index: the warrior wasp, the tarantula hawk wasp, and—most excruciating—the bullet ant, the pain of which is described as akin to walking over flaming coals with a 3-inch rusty nail stuck in your heel.

THE SCHMIDT INDEX

American entomologist Justin Orvel Schmidt began rating the pain caused by insect stings after experiencing a number of painful ones himself in the course of his research into Hymenoptera—stinging ants, wasps, and bees. His Schmidt Sting Pain Index, published in 1984, has been updated twice since—Schmidt has now been stung by some 150 different species.

The five-point index ranges from 0 to 4, with 0 defined as the feeling of being stung by an insect that cannot penetrate human skin and 4 an intensely painful sting. The bullet ant, *Paraponera clavata*, native to the tropical forests of Central America, is the world's largest ant species. Its venom contains poneratoxin, which causes sweats, nausea, and extreme pain. Bullet ants are generally not aggressive unless provoked—the venom evolved as a way to protect their colonies.

WHY DO INSECTS STING?

Bee, wasp, and ant stings are actually adapted from parts of their egg-laying anatomy, so usually only females sting. They use their sting as a weapon, to hunt and kill prey, protect their nests, and defend their lives against other predators. Hymenoptera are all descendants of a wasplike stinging ancestor that existed over 100 million years ago, so they're obviously doing something right.

36 WHY DO ELEPHANTS HAVE SUCH BIG EARS?

While all mammals have their evolutionary oddities, the elephant stands out for its size, its nose, and its large floppy ears. Unlike the auricular appendages of other warm-blooded animals, the elephant's ears are supersized. The reason? Their ears are how they stay cool.

HOT STUFF

The sheer size of an elephant means it produces a vast amount of metabolic heat. An elephant's skin alone cannot release that heat quickly enough, and those large, flat ears are essential. They're tightly packed with veins through which hot blood can pump and release the heat. However, this will only happen if the surrounding air is colder than 100°F, which isn't always the case in their natural habitat. To help with the cooling process, elephants seek out shade and never stray too far from water (although desert-dwelling elephants can go several days without it), often spraying water over their ears with their trunk to keep them wet. They also flap their ears, generating their own cooling breeze.

HORSES FOR COURSES

Where elephants live in cooler climates, such as India, their ears are noticeably smaller. Mammoths, which lived in the tundra regions of Siberia, had fur and thick layers of fat to stay warm, and—unlike their descendants—really small, furry ears.

37 WHY DO FLAMINGOS STAND ON ONE LEG?

Debate still rages about why flamingos spend much of their time—sometimes up to four hours at a stretch—balancing their body weight on one long, spindly leg. Suggested explanations range from camouflage among the surrounding reeds to just being more comfortable. However, it's widely agreed that it's about staying warm.

KEEPING COZY

Comparative psychologists Matthew Anderson and Sarah Williams observed that flamingos are more likely to stand on one leg while wading than when they're on land. They believe the reason is thermoregulation—when the flamingo is in the water, it loses more body heat by keeping both legs submerged, hence the balancing act.

LEFT- OR RIGHT-HEADED?

When Anderson and Williams set out to research the flamingo, they'd initially hoped to learn whether the bird has a preference for the side of its body it uses for specific tasks. They noticed that while flamingos do have a preference for which side they rest their heads (most rest their head to the right, in the same way most humans are right-handed), they don't seem to mind which side does the leg work. They also noted that the birds that went against the grain and rested their head on the left were likely to be more aggressive toward other birds.

REFLEX ACTION

Scientists in New Zealand may have found another reason entirely for the flamingo's one-legged lifestyle. They think the behavior might be more to do with a natural reflex than the temperature of the water. They found that it's likely flamingos share a primitive ability with whales and dolphins, which are able to shut down just part of their brain when they sleep in the water, to prevent them from drowning. If so, the action of tucking the leg up could be a result of them becoming drowsy—a natural reflex in line with how the bird would normally lower itself to the ground for sleep. The researchers believe this half-awake state allows them to rest while staying vigilant to predators.

PINK POOL PARTY

With their bright pink plumage, flamingos are one of the most recognizable birds in the world. But they don't start out that way—flamingo chicks have gray feathers. They develop their distinctive hue from their diet of algae and shrimp. These foods are rich in carotenoids, which are broken down in the liver into pigment molecules, and absorbed by fatty deposits in the feathers, legs, and even bill. This helps to explain the variance in color of flamingos in different parts of the world. Where flamingos are eating more algae, such as in the Caribbean, they are a richer, deeper color; but where their diet is made up of small creatures that feed on algae, they're usually a lighter pink.

38 CAN DOGS SMELL EMOTION?

Dogs' noses are wondrous things. Their acute sense of smell enables them to be trained to detect bombs and drugs, and find earthquake survivors. But it also makes them fine-tuned to human emotions, strengthening the bond between dog and owner and helping them serve as therapeutic companions to those in distress.

A NOSE OF TWO HALVES

Dogs have a unique nasal system. Unlike our rather basic noses, where breathing in and out occurs through the same part of the nostrils, dogs' noses have a clever slit at the sides, where the air passes out. This means they can build up the concentration of a particular scent by drawing more odor molecules into their nose more quickly. Inside their nose there are two separate areas—one for breathing and one for smelling. The smelling region features hundreds of millions of olfactory cells, compared to a human's meager ten million. These cells are what help to send electrical signals to the brain.

SENSE OF SMELL

It could be said that dogs are wired to smell. The portion of the canine brain dedicated to smell is significantly larger than the relative area used in a human brain. The damp, spongy surface area of the nose works to draw air molecules in. This, combined with the fact that dogs can smell through both nostrils separately, helps them to determine the direction a scent is coming from, and makes for a nose of epic capabilities. It can detect and interpret smells at concentrations 100 million times lower than a human can.

HOW ABOUT HORMONES?

On top of their super-sensitive sniffing skills, dogs are gifted with a particularly astute vomeronasal organ, which sits above the roof of their mouth. It is also known as the Jacobson's organ after its discoverer, anatomist Ludvig Levin Jacobson. Its primary function is to detect pheromones—chemical compounds, often without any discernible scent, that transmit signals between organisms of the same species. They help dogs to identify both potential mates and hostile threats from other animals. Studies have shown that dogs can also pick up on other animals' pheromones, including those of humans. These pheromone scents can help a dog detect a person's sex and age, and if a woman is pregnant.

Unfortunately, research into human pheromones is severely lacking. For example, while scientists have been able to identify two pheromones, androstenone and androstenol, that attract fertile female boars to their male counterparts, they've not been able to isolate a human equivalent. There is significant evidence from studies, such as babies being able to smell breast milk and adults being able to determine if a person is anxious or not by the smell of their sweat, that shows our pheromones give out signals, but apparently dogs are a lot more adept at reading them than we are.

39 WHICH ANIMALS CAN HAVE A VIRGIN BIRTH?

Until science fiction becomes science fact, humans still rely on mating to procreate, but for some species, asexual reproduction isn't some future possibility: it's happening right now.

THE BIRDS AND THE BEES

Finding the perfect mate can be tricky, which is why some animals have figured out how to have offspring without a partner. The process is called parthenogenesis, loosely translated from Greek to mean "virgin creation."

Typically, sexual reproduction involves two key ingredients: an egg cell and a sperm cell. Combined, they contain the genetic information required for a new living organism to develop. Parthenogenesis is different—the female of the species has a unique way of filling in the sperm-shaped gaps. There are two main types: automixis and apomixis. The former sees a by-product in egg cell production, called polar bodies, being merged with an egg to produce offspring. The process mixes up the mother's genes, so the resulting offspring are similar but not identical to the mother. In apomixis, more common in plants, the mother's egg cells replicate over and over without the genes being mixed up to create a genetically identical offspring—a clone.

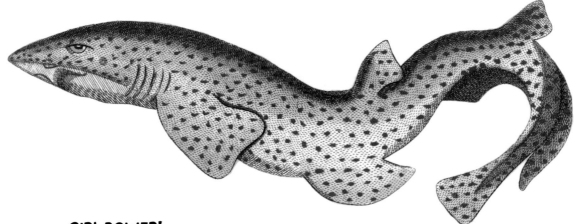

GIRL POWER!

Organisms that reproduce through automixis parthenogenesis tend to only create female offspring. That's because babies get two X chromosomes from their mother, rather than the option of a Y chromosome from a male partner, which kick-starts male development. Some insects can produce male offspring this way, but these males can only produce X-chromosome-containing sperm, so all their kids are females too.

IT'S A HARD KNOCKED-UP LIFE

These "virgin births" have been going on for millions of years in tiny organisms and small invertebrates like bees, wasps, ants, and other insects, but might be more recent in more advanced vertebrates. This evolutionary ability could be nature's way of helping animals survive in unfavorable conditions, particularly in deserts and on islands where mates might be hard to come by. By reproducing asexually, an animal doesn't have to waste energy finding a mate and can keep the species going. This does have its drawbacks, however, as the genetic similarity between individuals would make the whole population more vulnerable to disease.

SOMETHING FISHY

Scientists have observed this rare process in more than 80 vertebrate species, both in the wild and in captivity, including large lizards, snakes, and even sharks. In 2016, Leonie, a zebra shark at Reef HQ Aquarium in Australia, gave her keepers quite a shock when she laid three eggs that hatched into living shark pups, despite living in a tank with other females.

MAMMALIAN MURMURS

So what about humans? Despite the process being fairly widespread, it doesn't occur naturally in mammals. That's because genomic imprinting in mammals determines which genes are from the male and female partners respectively. With just one parent, some genes wouldn't be activated at all. But in 2004 scientists genetically engineered a mouse to have a virgin birth, so maybe artificial human parthenogenesis is not so far away.

40 WHAT IS THE WORLD'S LARGEST SINGLE ORGANISM?

How do you measure large? Tallest? Longest? Heaviest? If you consider weight alone, the blue whale—the world's largest animal—can tip the scale at 220 tons. Pretty big, you might think. But it pales in comparison to the heaviest single organism: a tree with the nickname Pando, Latin for "I spread."

THE ROOT OF THE MATTER

Made up of 47,000 tree trunks, and spanning 106 acres of Utah's Wasatch Mountains, is a quaking aspen that holds the title for the world's heaviest organism. Sharing a single root system and a unique set of genes, this extraordinary tree is believed to weigh an estimated 13 million pounds. That's significantly heavier than the world's largest giant sequoia, which weighs in somewhere around 4.5 million pounds.

While most trees reproduce using sexual reproduction (either through a male tree producing pollen in its flowers, which is then used to fertilize the flowers in a female tree, or a single tree fulfilling the roles of both sexes), some species, like the male quaking aspen, use vegetable reproduction. The tree sends out roots horizontally underground, up to distances of 100 feet. Shoots grow vertically from these roots, becoming stems and developing into new tree trunks, the tree thereby cloning itself many times over. Because of this connectedness, when a single stem dies the entire organism is affected by a hormonal imbalance. Multiple stem deaths lead to a huge increase in new stems as the tree attempts to make up the numbers.

FIVE QUICK FACTS

1 SLOTHS ARE SLOW AT EATING TOO

A sloth will take about two weeks to digest its dinner—with some taking up to 30 days—the longest digestive rate for any mammal. Their low metabolic rate means they can survive on relatively little food as well.

2 KOALAS COULD GET AWAY WITH CRIMES

The tree-dwelling marsupials have fingerprints uncannily similar to humans, so much so that it's likely investigators could confuse them at a crime scene.

3 BATS MAKE CHOCOLATE POSSIBLE

Without the world's only flying mammal, we wouldn't have cocoa (or bananas, avocados, or mangoes for that matter). Over 300 species of fruit depend on bats for pollination.

4 SOME WILD CHIMPS ENJOY A TIPPLE

Studies of wild chimpanzees in Guinea show they enjoy drinking fermented palm sap, and it's not hard to see why—it has an alcohol content of 3 percent.

5 ELEPHANTS CAN'T JUMP

Unlike other mammals, they don't need to. Their skeletons are designed with all their bones pointing straight down, which means they lack the upward spring required for jumping. And if they want to reach up high, their telescopic trunks are the perfect tool.

43 WHY DON'T GIRAFFES GET HEAD RUSHES?

With a 2-foot-long heart weighing up to 25 pounds and the highest known blood pressure of any mammal, you'd think simple tasks like taking a sip of water would make a giraffe quite woozy. But these impressive creatures have a unique cardiovascular system that renders those 15-foot head raises a breeze.

WHAT IS A HEAD RUSH?

The woozy feeling, often called a head rush, is caused by the effects of lowered blood pressure when you move too quickly from a seated or horizontal position to a vertical position. The body has built-in mechanisms to increase blood pressure, moving more blood from your legs and feet up to your head when you stand up, but if this doesn't happen effectively enough, you will feel light-headed.

BIG-HEARTED CREATURE

While a person's head is positioned about a foot from their heart, a giraffe's can be 7 feet away. Their enlarged hearts are designed to counteract this distance and the effects of gravity with power, pumping 16 gallons of blood per minute. This exceptionally high blood pressure is great for when the giraffe is bolt upright, feeding from the tops of trees, but what about when it bows down for a quick drink? Valves positioned in the main neck veins automatically close when the giraffe bends down, reducing the amount of blood traveling to the head. These veins grow thicker and stronger over time and have an elastic quality that enables them to expand and contract to accommodate the sudden changes in blood flow.

SOAK IT UP

The final flourish of this anatomical marvel is a spongelike web of veins at the base of the giraffe's brain, which helps to absorb and divert as much blood as possible when the head is lowered. Then, when the giraffe raises its head, the veins are able to quickly restore blood flow to the brain so the animal doesn't get light-headed on its quick ascent.

GIRAFFES IN SPACE

Giraffe physiology has been studied by NASA scientists to help them reduce the effects of a weightless environment on astronauts' blood vessels. In a similar way to space travelers, who spend most of the time with reduced blood pressure in their lower limbs, fetal giraffes' legs don't face much gravitational pull in the womb, but as soon as they're born things are very different. In the 1980s, scientists recorded how baby giraffes, which are normally on their feet 30 minutes after birth in the wild, quickly build their own gravity-defying suit. The blood vessels and skin in their legs thicken, so blood cannot pool there. These natural compression socks were instrumental in the development of NASA's Lower Body Negative Pressure Device, a treadmill contraption that applies negative pressure to the lower body while exercising in space, helping to prevent the loss of cardiovascular function and muscle.

44 CAN ANY PLANTS CALL FOR HELP WHEN THEY'RE BEING EATEN?

Plants have powerful defense mechanisms to protect them from predators. For example, when certain plants are bitten by insects, they detect toxic chemicals and in response release a chemical of their own which is toxic to the insect. But some plants need allies in the animal kingdom to help defend against attack.

THE SECRET LIFE OF PLANTS

Many studies have been made of *Nicotiana* species, otherwise known as tobacco plants. Their seeds can lie dormant for over a century, so they have to be extremely resilient and adaptive to their environment, never knowing what the next threat will be. Caterpillars that decide to tuck into one had better watch out, because their saliva causes the plant to produce airborne chemicals that attract a parasitic wasp. This wasp likes to lay its eggs inside the caterpillars; the larva feeds on the caterpillar as it grows, eventually killing it. This mutually beneficial relationship works out well for both the plant and the wasp (the caterpillar, not so much).

CALL OF THE WILD

Corn, tobacco, and cotton plants all send out chemicals to attract specific parasitic wasps that feed on the caterpillar species that's attacking them. Studies have found that commercial tobacco plants go one better by trying to minimize their chances of attack both day and night by making the most of whichever insects are up and about. Parasitic wasps hunt during the day, so plants call them for help when the sun's up, but when the plants are under attack at night, they emit a different chemical blend that deters nocturnal moths from laying eggs. This helps to keep the hungry caterpillar population down when the plant is most vulnerable.

TALKING TREES

Some plants, not content with chatting with the insect world, are able to communicate with other leafy species, too. While the study of plant communication is relatively recent, initial research looked into whether plants, intentionally or not, were capable of signaling to their own kind and other species, warning other plants of impending danger.

A 1980s study, "The Secret Life of Plants," became a huge sensation when it claimed that damaged maple and poplar trees released chemical cues that seemed to increase defenses in their undamaged neighbors. Over the years, research has been extended to a number of other plants, and food scientists are harnessing this new information to change the way crops are farmed. In East Africa, fields of corn are constantly under attack from stem-borer caterpillars. But if molasses grass is grown alongside the corn, the attacks are less catastrophic. The grass attracts a wasp that keeps the caterpillar population under control.

45 CAN CROCODILES CRY?

When someone fake-cries, we might describe it as "crocodile tears," but do the toothy creatures ever shed a tear? And what causes them to start sobbing?

LACHRYMOSA

The etymology of the term "crocodile tears" has been in use for centuries, based on an old myth that crocodiles weep while feasting on their prey—an act they can hardly be sad about. But it turns out that crocodiles really do have a good old cry while they chow down on their dinner. In 2007, researchers published a paper in *BioScience* titled "Crocodile Tears: And they eat them weeping." They had studied seven crocodilians of two different species feeding in captivity. To figure out whether they were generating tears or not, they fed them away from water. Five of the seven subjects developed bubbling or moisture in their eyes either before, during, or after they had eaten. The scientists suggested this was a result of the crocodile hissing and huffing while it eats—air was being pushed through the crocs' sinuses and on the eye, carrying secretions with it in the process.

TEARS AT TEATIME

Humans suffering from Bell's palsy—a facial nerve paralysis causing muscle weakness on one side of the face—have been known to tear up while eating. Known as "crocodile tears" or paradoxical lacrimation, the condition is caused when the facial nerve regenerates incorrectly, so when the sufferer chews they cry too. Unlike in crocodiles, who will forever look insincere while feasting, a shot of botulinum toxin treats humans with the condition.

46 WHY DO CROCODILES SWALLOW STONES?

While the typical crocodile diet would turn most human stomachs—frogs, mollusks, and rotting carcasses, anyone?—it's the side order of stones that is truly unappealing. Crocs are one of a few creatures in the animal kingdom to swallow stones. And they don't do this by accident.

DIGESTIVE DIRT

When stones are swallowed, they are known as gastroliths. And there are a few reasons crocodiles do this—these rocky ready-meals are really rather useful.

First, they can aid a crocodile's digestion. Rocks in the stomach help to grind up food, which is particularly helpful when you're not taking the time to chew. Crocodiles have been known to eat large animals whole, so the gastroliths help to break down the bones and shells of their prey. Some scientists also think the rocks help the crocodile to feel fuller when prey is scarce.

WEIGHTY MEAL

Crocodiles spend a significant amount of time underwater, or with only their eyes and nostrils visible, stalking their prey. The added weight of 10 or 15 pounds from gastroliths can help to weigh them down under the water. Some scientists think the increase in body weight is not significant enough to affect buoyancy, but that the rocks have more of a stabilizing effect, so the croc is less likely to roll from side to side in the water.

47 WHAT'S SPECIAL ABOUT A LUNGFISH'S LUNG?

When it comes to staying alive, the African lungfish is something of a pro. The eel-like fish is a "living fossil," having been inhabiting rivers and lakes of West Africa for nearly 400 million years.

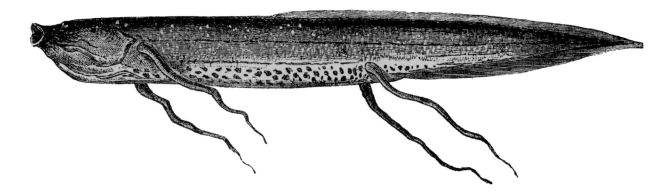

BREATHE IT IN

Lungfishes are named for their primitive lung, a biological adaptation that they have developed over time to help them survive in the region's extreme climate. They have gills that extract oxygen from the water, but every 30 minutes or so the lungfish will rise to the surface to extract oxygen from the air instead. This means that when the rainy season passes and the rivers dry up, they don't have to rely on water to survive. For up to two years they can live in a state of estivation, a type of hibernation.

A FISH IN MUCK

As the river and lakebeds dry, they burrow about 10 inches below the surface. Their mouths act as a shovel, chewing through the mud and spewing it out through its gills, creating a little burrow. There, the lungfish spits out mucus, which solidifies, creating a small sheltered habitat that can trap moisture while letting in air from above. Typically, these omnivorous fish eat mollusks, tree roots, frogs, and other fish. But to survive their lengthy stay in the food-free mud, the fish doesn't burn fat like most hibernating animals. Instead it digests its own muscle tissue to absorb nutrients.

QUIZ
ANIMALS AND PLANTS

Think you've got the birds and bees all figured out?
Make sure you're top of the class with this quick quiz.

QUESTIONS:

1. Which long-necked animal has special valves in its neck veins to prevent it from getting a head rush?

2. What is the bullet ant best known for: its speed or its painful sting?

3. A dog's Jacobson's organ would be found in its tail—true or false?

4. What is the world's largest animal?

5. Parakeets are a species of which type of bird, known for their mimicking abilities?

6. Crocodiles swallow stones to weigh them down—true or false?

7. In relation to their average body size, are dolphins' brains large or small?

8. What makes flamingos pink?

9. Lungfish digest their own tissue to absorb nutrients. True or false?

10. What was the name of the shark who hatched triplets, despite living in a tank of other females?

Turn to page 245 for the answers.

ANCIENT HISTORY

48 HOW DID THE INCAS BUILD MACHU PICCHU SO HIGH UP?

Set in a tropical mountain forest in the Amazonian Andes, 8,000 feet above sea level, Machu Picchu is a 15th-century architectural marvel. It might seem odd to choose to build a stone fortress at such a high altitude—but nestled at the top of that mountain was a quarry of white granite.

STONE ON STONE

The Historic Sanctuary of Machu Picchu, a UNESCO World Heritage Site, was built in the classical Inca style of the period. The whole site covers 80,536 acres, and centers around the structure at the top of the mountain, La Ciudadela—the citadel. The entire complex was meticulously planned before the first piece of granite was cut from the quarry. The quarry wasn't the only reason the site was selected. Its sacred relevance (the Incas believed it was close to the sun god), spectacular views, and nearby natural spring, which served as the community's water supply, all played a part.

MAGIC STEPS

Key to the build's success were the city's foundations. The Incas knew the site had to be able to withstand high rainfall—79 inches every year—and the weight of the planned structures. A deep foundation was dug out for over 600 terraces, most of which were hidden underground. Retaining walls that leaned inward provided stability for the terrace system, preventing the city from sliding off the mountain. The walls were filled in with layers of large rocks, smaller rocks, sandy gravel, and topsoil,

allowing rainwater and groundwater to drain through the terraces. A typical terrace was built about 7 feet high by 10 feet wide. They are the reason the site remains so well preserved despite 400 years of neglect, working like claws to cling to the mountain. They also provided a place to grow crops for the isolated community.

ROCK AROUND THE CLOCK

Hundreds of thousands of stones were used to build around 200 structures, including several temples, 600 terraces, 16 fountains, and thousands of steps. The stones, which came from a number of nearby quarries, weighed up to 14 tons and measured up to 9 feet long. Without the modern benefit of motorized equipment, or even animals or wheeled carts to move the stones, the Incas made ingenious use of leverage, placing logs beneath the rocks and pushing them in unison. They also had ramps made from earth that they could move into place to help push a stone uphill. The Incas had no iron tools—the precise stonework, which rivals modern production methods, was achieved using a hammer stone to carve the rock.

It is thought that a wooden-wedge technique was also used to break up larger rocks. Holes would be drilled into the rock and wet wood inserted; the water in the wood would then freeze and expand, splitting the rock apart. And the Incas didn't use any kind of mortar to hold the wall together. The rocks were cut accurately, often with indentations that would lock together.

49 WHY WAS IT SO HARD TO POISON A ROMAN EMPEROR?

Since the age of a great Roman enemy, Mithridates VI Eupator, King of Pontus (120–63 BC), emperors routinely poisoned themselves to build up immunity to the very real threat of assassination, making it very difficult to kill them by this method.

PICK YOUR POISON

The Romans lived in murderous times— mass poisonings were not unheard of—and no one was more at risk than the rich and powerful rulers. While animal and mineral poisons were occasionally used, such as cantharidin from beetles or mercury and arsenic, the most common way to bring about a rival's death was through vegetable poisons. These included belladonna alkaloids, found in deadly nightshade, which causes hallucinations and convulsions; aconite from wolf's bane, a large dose of which could bring about sudden death; and hemlock, which attacks the central nervous system, causing seizures and respiratory failure.

RECIPE TO RULE BY

Mithridates was considered one of the greatest kings of his time and could apparently speak 25 languages. He had a keen interest in medicine and developed several antidotes, which tended to contain unusual ingredients such as duck blood. One antidote, made up of a number of poisonous substances, took his name and became popular with those who succeeded him: mithridatium. While researchers are uncertain exactly what the antidote would have contained, one recipe recorded by Roman author Pliny included two nuts, two figs, 20 leaves of the herb rue, and a pinch of salt: "He who took this fasting would be immune to all poison for that day."

50 HOW DID THE AZTECS KEEP FIT?

The Aztecs, or Mexica as they called themselves, lived in what is now Central America, and are best known for their impressive architecture and for being wiped out by smallpox. But their highly developed culture and customs included mandatory schooling for children, keeping tax records, intricate art, and their own popular sport.

through their ring first was the winner. This was notoriously difficult, as the ball could only come into contact with players' knees, forearms, head, feet, hips, buttocks, and elbows. Their hands, calves, and even the floor were out of play. In parts of Mexico a game called *ulama*, which bears many similarities to this ancient sport, is still played today.

ROLL THE STONES

A less energetic pastime was *patolli*. Similar to contemporary dice games like pachisi and ludo, with its cross-shaped board, red bean counters, and stone die, this was a game of chance and skill popular with nobles and commoners alike. The aim was to move your counters from one end of the board to the other, with several people able to play at once. Gambling was common, with some people even gambling themselves into servitude.

GAME OF TWO HOOPS

When the Mexica settled somewhere new, one of the first things to be constructed was a *tlachtli*—a court with two facing walls, where people played *ullamaliztli*. On each wall was a ring with six pegs on either side. Players on two teams would then attempt to get a rubber ball, called a *ulli*, through the ring. Points were awarded for knocking out the pegs, and the team to get the ball

51 WHAT SPORTS DID THEY PLAY AT THE ANCIENT GREEK OLYMPICS?

Historical records date the first ancient Olympic games to 776 BC. The games were originally held every four years in Olympia, in southwestern Greece, with competitors traveling from across the region's various states. The very first Olympics lasted just one day and had a single event—a sprint race.

NO BITING, NO POKING

Over time, more events were added. Between 396 BC and the first century AD, the games spanned five days, including an opening and closing ceremony, a mass slaughter of a hundred oxen, a funeral ceremony in honor of a mythological hero, and a day of prayer. There were lots of sports, but no team events: everyone competed as an individual. Events included three running distances on a wide track where 20 people could run side by side, wrestling, boxing, horse and chariot races, and the pentathlon—as well as a five-event competition comprising running, long jump, discus, javelin, and wrestling. One of the toughest sports was the pankration—a primitive martial art that combined wrestling and boxing. Biting and poking out people's eyes were banned, but this largely rules-free sport could get ugly.

WHAT DID THEY WIN?

The ancient Olympic games were the inspiration for the modern Olympics, which began in 1896. Unlike today's victors, who receive a bronze, silver, or gold medal depending on their ranking, ancient Greek Olympians were all fighting to be the sole winner of each event—the *Olympionike*. Immediately after the event finished, the winner would be presented with a palm leaf by a judge. The crowd would applaud and throw flowers, and tie red skeins of wool around the hands and head of the victor. At the end of the whole contest an official prize ceremony took place in the Temple of Zeus. All the victors would be presented with a crown of olive branches, known as a *kotinos*.

Just as today's athletes often receive victory parades and lucrative endorsement deals on their return from the Olympics, the same was true for Greek *Olympionikes*, who were welcomed home as heroes by their city-states. Songs would be written in their honor, and if an athlete had won three events, he could commission a leading sculptor to create a portrait statue to commemorate his success. Many athletes were sponsored by the state, which paid for such privileges, as their heroes' sporting achievements brought great prestige to their hometown.

FOR THE GODS

While the ancient games were, like today's games, an exhibition of strength and endurance, they also had an underlying religious significance for the ancient Greeks. Iphitos, the king of the state where Olympia was situated, established the games to calm the anger of the gods and bring peace to the region. The games were organized in honor of Zeus, the king of the gods. And in some sense, peace was a big part of the event. The *Ekecheiria*, or "Olympic truce," meant that city-states were obliged to stop fighting for a month to allow the 40,000 athletes, spectators, and tradespeople from all over the country to travel safely to the event.

52 WHAT WAS THE EARLIEST HUMAN RIGHTS CHARTER?

In the British Museum resides an object called the Cyrus Cylinder. It dates from 539 BC and is named for Cyrus the Great, the Persian ruler who founded the Achaemenid dynasty. This ancient artifact points to the first civilization willing to document the rights of its citizens—paving the way for the freedoms we cherish today.

CYRUS CYLINDER

The clay-baked cylinder was created, most likely on Cyrus's orders, after his peaceful invasion of the fabled city of Babylon. It's engraved in Babylonian script, and the writings tell the story of how Cyrus was chosen by Marduk, the city-god of Babylon, to take the city after Nabonidus, the last king of Babylon, had imposed work on all the city's people. The etchings talk about Cyrus's just and peaceful rule, his abolition of the forced labor practice, and how he returned deported people to the city, leading many to see it as an ancient precursor to the human rights charters that would follow.

MAGNA CARTA

While it came many centuries after the Cyrus Cylinder, the Magna Carta's principles underpin many of the laws, constitutions, and charters that have followed it, including the Universal Declaration of Human Rights. Issued in 1215 by King John of England and revised throughout the 13th century, the Magna Carta established important principles such as the fact that every man was subject to the rule of law and that every free man should have the right to justice and a fair trial.

53 HOW MANY SECRETS DID EMPEROR QIN SHI HUANG TAKE TO THE GRAVE?

At the northern foot of Lishan Mountain, in Shaanxi Province, is the burial site of China's first emperor, Qin Shi Huang. Discovered by well-digging farmers in 1974, the complex, believed to be the largest and most opulent of its kind, contains some 600 individual sites around a central grave mound.

TREASURE TROVE

Archaeologists and historians have theorized that workers from all corners of the empire worked for nearly four decades to create this underground city, covering around 22 square miles. From the sites that have been excavated so far, it would appear the emperor, who died in 210 BC, aged 39, was buried near to everything he would need in the afterlife. Two thousand terra-cotta soldiers, each unique in style and expression, are believed to be part of an eight thousand-strong army. Archaeologists have also unearthed horses, chariots, and weapons in the small part of the site they've managed to excavate. Pits believed to contain concubines and an elaborate palace have yet to be unearthed.

MERCURY RISING

However, the secrets of the burial mound itself—which rises out of the flat landscape to a height of 168 feet—remain a mystery. The Chinese government is likely waiting until technology is able to ensure preservation of its contents—earlier excavations of the terra-cotta warriors led to their paint peeling off—and the safety of those who enter. Writings from the ancient historian Sima Qian refer to mercury rivers inside the tomb, representing the Yangtze and the Yellow River, as well as traps that would fire arrows at any intruders.

54 HOW DID THE ROMANS TURN DEATH INTO DAYTIME ENTERTAINMENT?

The Romans loved spectacle, and nowhere was this more apparent than in the public shows organized by their rulers. To remain in favor, Rome's emperors built vast venues, including the famous Colosseum and Circus Maximus, where animal hunts, public executions, and even naval battles were staged—at the cost of many human lives.

LUDI MERIDIANI

Held in the empire's amphitheaters at midday, after the animal hunts (venationes) and before the gladiatorial battles, the ludi meridiani were considered a necessary form of social control. These public executions showed the people that the powers that be were running the show. Condemned criminals were the unlucky "performers" in this spectacle, where they could face a number of horrifying ends. Those sentenced to death would be led into the arena partially clothed or completely naked, and often shackled to await their fate. This could come in the form of wild animals, an executioner (confector), or a fight to the death with other prisoners. In "fatal charades," these unlucky souls were forced to reenact mythical stories before they were killed.

WATER SPORTS

The naumachia, or water shows, were extreme even for the Romans. While some naumachia took place in the Colosseum itself, flooded with water, many of these epic reenactments were held in costly artificial basins built specially for the event. One impressive show put on by Augustus in 2 BC saw 30 ships re-create the Battle of Salamis (480 BC), with 3,000 men fighting to the death. It was set in a basin that measured approximately 445 feet by 1,170 feet— around the length of five football fields— and filled with about 460,000 cubic yards of water. That's enough to fill more than 100 Olympic-size swimming pools.

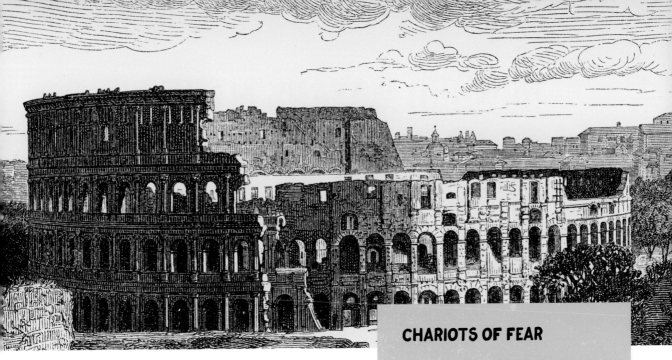

The men who played the parts of oarsmen and soldiers in these shows were usually prisoners of war or criminals. In another water show, staged by Julius Caesar in 46 BC, 4,000 oarsmen rowed 2,000 soldiers into the fake battle, dressed in costumes as Egyptians and Tyrians. But while the battle was largely choreographed to reflect history, the fighting was real. Thousands died, either in combat or by drowning, to keep the Roman hordes entertained.

CHARIOTS OF FEAR

For those interested in fame and glory, chariot racing was the way to go. Gladiators, while popular with the crowds, had low social status, no different from prostitutes or actors. But charioteers were treated like heroes and famed throughout the Roman world. That's if you survived. Chariot racing was notoriously dangerous, with races seeing four charioteers speeding around the track while controlling two or four horses at once. The men would wrap the reins tightly around their wrists, so in the event of a collision they had to make a snap judgment whether to cut themselves free and risk being trampled by whatever was behind, or be dragged by their own horses into the fray. It's no surprise that many died pursuing their sport. The average age of death listed on charioteers' tombstones is just 22.

55 HOW DID MAYANS MAKE SURE THEIR BABIES WERE AT THE HEIGHT OF FASHION?

New parents today can spend a fortune kitting out their baby—but contemporary culture pales in comparison to the lengths taken by ancient Mayans to ensure their offspring were in vogue, from shaping their babies' heads to redirecting their gaze.

HEADS SHAPED LIKE CORN

Mayan concepts of beauty were heavily rooted in religious beliefs. The corn god, Yum Kaax, provided the inspiration for the sloped shape of their foreheads—as the elongated shape of an ear of corn narrows toward the top. This sloped head shape was created by artificial cranial deformation. Babies' head bones are relatively soft at birth to enable them to pass through the birth canal. The Mayan tradition took advantage of this, by binding a newborn's head between two wooden boards—one behind, and the other attached at an angle on top. The angle of the top board would be gradually reduced over several days to achieve the desired shape. Skeletal analysis of burial sites indicates that up to 90 percent of the population had endured this procedure as infants. Studies of skeletons found in Australia, the Bahamas, and Germany show that the Mayans weren't the only ancient civilization to meddle with their children's heads.

EYES ON THE PRIZE

But for the truly dedicated parent, there were other lengths you could go to. Another highly desirable feature was slightly crossed eyes. To achieve this effect, parents would tie small, soft balls or tiny stones to strands of their child's hair and position them in the center of their face. Over time this could cause their gaze to become crossed.

TEETHING PROBLEMS

Many adult Mayans would file their teeth either to a point or a T-shape, again thought to imitate the shape of a corn kernel. As wealthier children grew into adulthood, they would have holes drilled into the front of their teeth, which were then inset with precious stones such as jade, obsidian, or hematite. The stones were kept in place with a plant-based adhesive so strong that many of them have been found in skulls by archaeologists today.

FIVE QUICK FACTS

1 THE ANCIENT EGYPTIANS INVENTED TOOTHPASTE

Egyptians banished bad breath for good with a paste made from rock salt, pepper, mint, and dried iris flowers.

2 PEOPLE HAVE BEEN MONITORING EARTHQUAKES SINCE AD 130

The seismoscope (the seismograph's older sister) was invented by Zhang Heng, a Chinese astronomer. It could pinpoint the general location of an earthquake.

3 MUMMIFICATION WAS FIRST PRACTICED IN SOUTH AMERICA

The Chinchorro people would peel back a corpse's skin, remove the muscles and organs, and fill it with plants before sewing everything up. They were doing this 2,000 years before the Egyptians.

4 WE HAVE HORSE-RIDERS TO THANK FOR TROUSERS

Nomadic Central Asian herders in the 13th to 10th centuries BC invented some of the world's first trousers to make it easier to ride their horses. They were made from wool and had a roomy crotch and strings to fasten them at the waist.

5 ROMAN WOMEN TOOK A FORM OF CONTRACEPTION

The herb silphium was used so much—for contraception, abortion, as well as to treat everything from coughs to leprosy—that it became extinct by the first century BC.

56 WHAT WERE THE GREEKS' MOST DANGEROUS WEAPONS?

The Greeks spent much of their time fighting each other, as ancient Greece was not a country but a number of separate states, including the main city-states of Athens, Sparta, Corinth, Megara, and Argos. This means they had a lot of practice coming up with clever ways to defeat their enemies.

SPARTAN SOLDIERS

Some of these states were known for their formidable armies, none more so than Sparta. An old adage was that one Spartan soldier was worth several other Greek men. From the age of seven, all Spartan boys endured 13 years of training, known as the *agoge*, so they could fight for their city-state. Unlike other states' armies, which were drawn from men of various professions, Spartan men had one job for life, whether they liked it or not. Other roles in society were carried out by women, *helots* (slaves), and the *perieoci* (neither slaves nor citizens, these were craftsmen).

The Spartans were known for their spear, called a *dory*, which featured a bronze or iron spearhead at one end and a spike at the other. Known as the "lizard killer," this spike came in handy for standing the spear upright, finishing off any fallen enemies as the army marched over their dying bodies, and, of course, for killing lizards. The soldiers also carried a *xiphos*—a short sword that could be used to reach through the gaps in enemy shield walls, unlike the larger, unwieldy weapons of their foes.

RULING THE WAVES

Some Greek states, such as Athens, Corinth, and Rhodes, commanded the Mediterranean Sea with enormous fleets of warships. The ships enabled them to transport soldiers, protect their colonies, and build trading routes. The trireme was the most common of these ships and required 170 men to row it. The trireme's not-so-secret weapon was the sharp metal ram fixed to the front of it. It enabled the vessel to get close to an enemy ship, with the aim of crashing into it, causing severe damage and flooding.

INVENTING FEAR

Archimedes (ca. 287–212 BC) was born in the Greek colony of Syracuse. He devoted his life to philosophy, mathematics, and inventing. When the Romans conquered Syracuse in 211 BC, it was after a long and bitter siege in which Archimedes was instrumental. He was responsible for constructing the heaviest catapult ever built, capable of firing a 180-pound stone, and a mirror system that focused the sun's rays on enemy boats, setting them on fire. Archimedes was eventually killed by a Roman soldier, reportedly while in the middle of some absorbing calculations.

QUICK FACT

FIRE AND BRIMSTONE

One dangerous weapon wrongly attributed to the Greeks, but actually invented by the Greek-speaking Byzantine citizens of the eastern Roman Empire in the seventh century AD is "Greek fire." Thought to have been a petroleum-based mixture, Greek fire was launched from flame-throwing tubes on ships, igniting enemy vessels and soldiers.

57 COULD YOU GET A PRENUP IN ANCIENT EGYPT?

We tend to think of women's rights, in most cultures, as a relatively new thing. In ancient Egypt, however, women enjoyed a parity with men in most aspects of life. With divorce a possibility, the option of a premarital agreement or divorce contract provided women with power and security unmatched in other ancient cultures.

CONTRACTUAL OBLIGATIONS

At the Oriental Institute of the University of Chicago hangs a 2,480-year-old Egyptian annuity contract that promises the wife 1.2 pieces of silver and 36 bags of grain every year for the rest of her life, with or without her husband. Other existing legal documents from the time show a woman's personal possessions and finances recorded, so that her husband would know what to repay her in case of divorce. Women were also entitled to one-third of any of their husband's wealth that was acquired during their marriage.

GIRL POWER

Egyptian women often had to rely on men financially, as employment was one area where they did not enjoy parity with men. But, regardless of their marital status, they did have many legal rights. They could serve on juries and as witnesses in court, could sue and be sued, and even own their own property, including slaves, lands, and goods. Women would often make money by growing vegetables, making clothing, and even renting out their own slaves, which they often clubbed together in consortiums to make them affordable.

QUIZ
ANCIENT HISTORY

Are you having a Roman holiday or is it still all Greek to you? Test yourself with this quick quiz to find out how much you've learned.

QUESTIONS:

1. Which of the following sports was not featured at the ancient Olympics: chariot races, wrestling, kayaking?

2. The Incas dragged vast quantities of stone up the mountainside to build Machu Picchu—true or false?

3. Why did Roman emperors routinely poison themselves?

4. Is the Magna Carta a cathedral, a sacred cart, or a famous document?

5. How much water was in the basin in which Augustus's famous *naumachia* (water show) took place in 2 BC—enough to fill a bucket, a bathtub, or more than 100 Olympic-size swimming pools?

6. Which body parts did Mayans alter to honor their god of corn?

7. What were the terra-cotta warriors guarding?

8. Ancient Egyptian women were entitled to all their husband's wealth if they divorced—true or false?

9. *Ullamaliztli* and *patolli* were games played by which ancient civilization?

10. Spartan men were automatically committed to what profession?

Turn to page 246 for the answers.

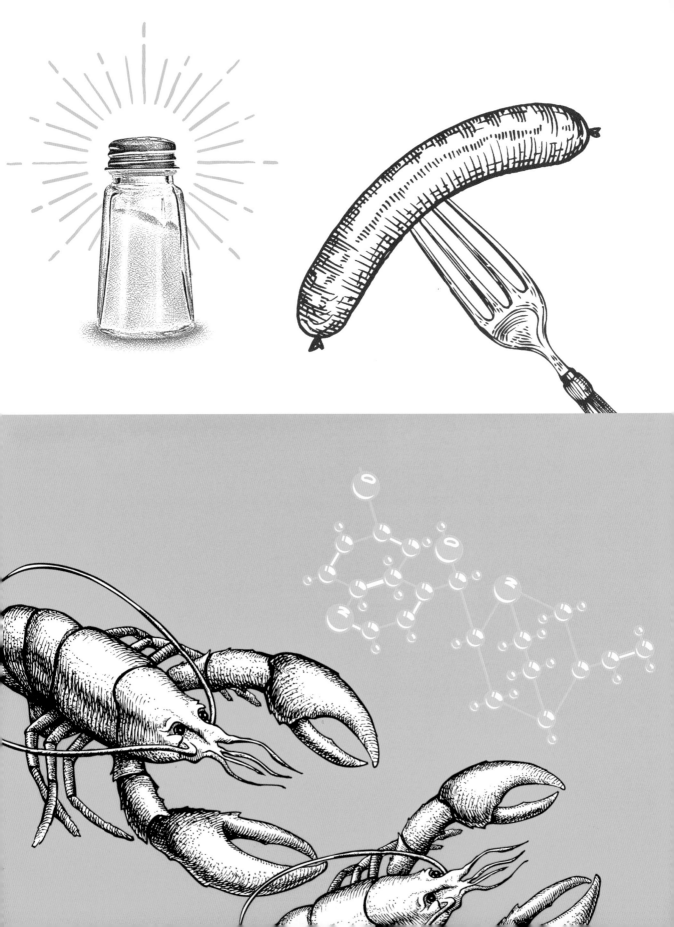

FOOD AND DRINK

58 WERE ROMAN SOLDIERS PAID IN SALT?

The word *salarium* was introduced during Augustus's rule of the Roman Empire. It means a salary, everything a person needs to survive, and is derived from the Latin word for salt, *sal*, as this was essential to Roman life. But were hardworking Roman soldiers paid in salt instead of money?

SEASONED TALE

A *salarium* was given to soldiers, military officers, and provincial governors and was to account for all the provisions they needed—clothing, weapons, and food, including salt. Soldiers did not buy these items, but their cost was deducted from the *salarium*. Any cash left over, usually about 20 percent, was paid to the soldiers in coins for them to spend as they wished.

THE VALUE OF SALT

The first great Roman road, the Via Salaria, leads from Rome to the saline-rich Adriatic Sea. Salt was a precious commodity whose price was heavily controlled by the Roman Empire—it was increased to raise money for wars, then lowered to enable even the poorest people to afford this essential item. Carts filled with salt would travel along this eponymous road and all over the empire to serve all manner of purposes.

Salt was not only a food additive and preservative (see opposite page), but also an antiseptic—it shares its Roman name in part with the goddess of health, Salus—and even a currency. Cato (95–46 BC), a politician during the Roman Republic, made a provision of salt for his slaves of about 0.7 ounce per day. It's unlikely a slave would have eaten this much salt, but it was probably traded with others.

It's also believed some slaves were bought and sold for salt, probably the origin of the saying "worth his salt." Later biblical references to salt also emphasize its high value. In the book of Matthew, Jesus said, "You are the salt of the earth" to his disciples to illustrate how cherished they were.

SALTY LANGUAGE

"Salt" or *sal* features as the root of many other Latin words and phrases—another sign of its importance in everyday life. "Salad" is derived from *salata*, meaning salted things, because salt was used to season vegetables. Salt was also associated with fertility, possibly because fish, which live in the salty sea, were known to reproduce far more than land animals. The Romans used the word *salax* to describe a man in love, literally referring to him as being in a salted state.

PASS THE SALT

Salt's preservative effects meant it held an important place in Roman kitchens. Salt was available in a number of different forms— there were golden-colored salts from Cappadocia in central Turkey and even darker varieties that had absorbed flavors from dried wood. The Romans, even by our modern salty standards, consumed a lot of the stuff. In *Apicius*—a collection of Roman culinary recipes, believed to be compiled in the fourth or fifth century AD—one recipe suggests cooking a suckling pig in a pot with its own weight in salt.

59 WHAT'S THE WORLD'S SPICIEST FOOD?

The Scoville scale measures the "heat" or piquancy of chilies—the spiciest food on Earth. The capsaicin molecule binds to pain receptors in the mouth, causing the eyes to water, the nose to run, and the skin to sweat in an effort to rid the body of this toxin.

SPICE THINGS UP

There are a few chilies that are universally agreed to be the hottest of the hot. These include the Bhut jolokia, or ghost pepper, used by the Indian military as a hand grenade ingredient; the Trinidad moruga scorpio and the Carolina Reaper, which became the Guinness World Record holder in 2013 for being the hottest chili. It averages 1.57 million Scoville Heat Units (SHU) on the scale, compared to the jalapeño's measly average of 2,500–8,000.

SCALING UP

Invented by pharmacist Wilbur Scoville in 1912, the Scoville Organoleptic Test is not an exact science. The highly subjective test involves a measured amount of capsaicin oil, extracted from a dried chili pepper, gradually being added to sugar water in decreasing concentrations. When three of a panel of five trained tasters can no longer detect the chili in the sample, then its SHU value is agreed. A bell pepper has a rating of zero SHU.

More recently, high-performance liquid chromatography has been used instead to measure chili strength and is considered more reliable. In this mass transfer process, a liquid containing the chili sample is pressurized and then pumped through a column that separates the sample's various components, allowing researchers to measure the precise levels of capsaicin. If you're brave enough, why not sample Blair's 16 Million Reserve—made from pure capsaicin crystals.

BRANCHING OUT

There are a couple of chemical compounds that feature higher than capsaicin on the Scoville scale. One is tinyatoxin, 331 times hotter than pure capsaicin, and the other, three times hotter than that, is resiniferatoxin. But you might have to settle for your mind being blown, rather than your mouth, because these are found only in two cactuslike plants native to Morocco and northern Nigeria.

FIVE QUICK FACTS

 A GAMBLING PROBLEM LED TO THE BIRTH OF THE SANDWICH

The word "sandwich" and its popularity in England began in 1762, when John Montagu, the fourth Earl of Sandwich, wanted a snack he could enjoy while spending many hours at the card table.

 CHOCOLATE IS MORE VALUABLE THAN YOU THINK

Before cash and credit cards, ancient Mayan and Aztec civilizations in Central and South America used the cacao bean as a system of money.

 THE FIRST FOOD COOKED IN A MICROWAVE WAS POPCORN

Percy Spencer was developing transmitters during World War II when he noticed a chocolate bar in his pocket was melting from the radar. He created the first microwave oven in 1945 and used it to cook popcorn first and then an egg.

 LEMONS FLOAT IN WATER BUT LIMES SINK

That's because lemons have around the same density as water, and their rinds are covered in tiny air pockets, helping them float on water. Limes are denser than water, so although they're smaller, they sink more easily.

 RAW OYSTERS MIGHT STILL BE ALIVE WHEN THEY'RE EATEN

Freshly killed oysters taste better, but when an oyster's shucked to be eaten—that's when its abductor muscle is separated from its shell so it can't open or close it—it's not always killed. Since oysters are largely immobile, it can be hard to tell when they're dead.

60 WHAT GIVES CHEWING GUM ITS CHEW?

Most chewing gum is made from flavorings, colorings, preservatives, sweeteners, and a synthetic gum base. It's the base, the insoluble part of the product, that gives gum its unique "chew." Each manufacturer uses a recipe of food-grade polymers, waxes, and softeners to create their product's texture.

POLY-WHAT NOW?

A polymer is essentially a string of molecules, containing carbon and hydrogen. The ones in gum base are man-made, but they're identical in structure to polymers found in nature—and chewing gum's origins were actually natural. Humans have been chewing on something since time immemorial. Pliny the Elder (AD 23–79) once wrote about a plant-based derivative called *mastich*, enjoyed by the ancient Greeks, while Native Americans chewed spruce tree resin.

PROTECTIVE GUM

In the mid-1850s, Thomas Adams, a New York inventor, was helping the exiled Mexican president, Antonio López de Santa Anna, to develop a form of rubber using chicle resin from the sapodilla tree. The resin acts as a natural bandage, healing wounds in the tree's bark. Adams was unsuccessful, but soon realized he could use the resin as a base to develop a better form of chewing gum (prior to this, commercial chewing gum contained spruce resin or paraffin wax). The result was Chiclets—a candy-coated gum that's still available today. Synthetic polymers, which provided higher-quality and more consistent results, were widely used by the mid-1900s. It was just as well, because the rise in popularity for gum saw 25 percent of Mexico's sapodilla forests destroyed by 1930.

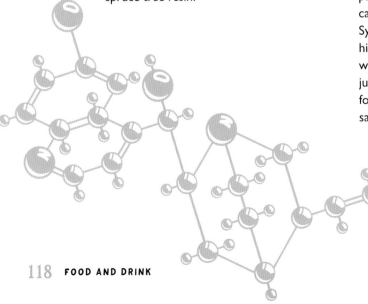

61 WHO INVENTED SLICED BREAD?

Bread is consumed around the world in an array of portable forms, from French croissants and Polish bagels to Ethiopian *injera* and Indian *paratha*. It's the ultimate convenience food—but an American baker decided it wasn't quite convenient enough.

SLICE OF SUCCESS

In 1928 a bakery in Chillicothe, Missouri, put the world's first commercially sliced loaves on sale. Otto Rohwedder was on a quest to bring the American people a more convenient form of their favorite starch. Although he'd taken great care to calculate housewives' optimum slice thickness—just under half an inch—bakers were still skeptical. They were concerned pre-sliced loaves would go stale more quickly, and they did. Rohwedder's solution was to insert a U-shaped pin into each end of the loaf to help it hold its shape and stay fresher. The "power-driven, multi-blade" bread slicer was a success, and led to the English phrase to describe future great ideas: "the best thing since sliced bread."

WARTIME RATIONS

During World War II, a wartime effort to conserve resources saw a ban on steel-produced bread-slicing machines in the United States. The ban was so unpopular, however, that it was lifted after just two months. In Britain, where white flour was usually imported from abroad, the government introduced a "national wheatmeal loaf," which utilized the entire wheat grain, including the husks. It was an unpopular staple throughout the rationing years. Meanwhile, in Germany, the Nazi regime introduced *Kriegsbrot*—"war bread"—made of rye, wheat, and potato flour (occasionally mixed with sawdust) to keep people sated.

62 WHAT IS THE WORLD'S MOST STOLEN FOOD?

If you had to have a Gouda guess as to which food gets pilfered the most, you'd probably say wine, whiskey, or maybe Wagyu beef, but you'd brie wrong. It's actually that smelliest of all foodie delights: cheese.

THE BIG CHEESE

In 2011 the UK's Centre for Retail Research found that cheese is the most stolen food globally, followed by meat. The research covered retail theft—including by employees, organized crime rings, and petty criminals— in 250,000 stores in 43 countries. According to the report, 4 percent of the world's cheese ends up being stolen, which makes it a high-risk item for retailers.

PARMIGIANO PLOT

Some cheeses are worth more than others, as one clandestine group of criminals discovered. The 11-strong gang started traveling around central and northern Italy to find factories and warehouses stocking wheels of the region's iconic Parmigiano-Reggiano cheese. And over the course of two years they were able to steal at least 2,039 wheels of the stuff. Known as the "King of all Cheeses," this unpasteurized cow's milk delicacy, with its strict production and quality criteria, is sought after by chefs and foodies around the world. A single wheel of this cheesy delight can sell for up to $500.

This was no cheesy string at a local supermarket. The men were armed with weapons and radios, had tools to break into the buildings they targeted, and special electronics to get around alarm systems. And for a while their illegal efforts paid off. After they were arrested in 2015, as part of Operation Wine and Cheese, Italian authorities estimate they stole somewhere in the region of $875,000 worth of the aged specialty.

EDAMMIT!

Perishable items like cheese pose a bigger risk to criminals looking to shift their booty on to other retailers and venues. Cheese thieves in Wisconsin found this out the hard way. In 2016, 70,000 pounds of cheese was stolen from a store in Germantown. Shortly after, it was recovered in Milwaukee. The thieves had clearly picked up the cheese-filled trailer without a clear plan of how they were going to shift its contents. Red flags were raised as soon as they started trying to sell cheese on the cheap without revealing its source—something that's tracked by law—and retailers wouldn't touch it. Even though the cheese was recovered, it all had to be disposed of because the thieves had broken the food inspector's seal when they opened the truck, making it unfit for sale.

QUICK FACT

THE PERFECT FORMULA

In Europe, cheese theft is big business, whereas in the United States, nonperishable, more expensive items tend to see higher theft rates. Baby formula is one such commodity, coveted because of its price tag and the fact it can be used to dilute narcotics, so is sought after by illegal drug manufacturers.

63 WHY DID PRISONERS USED TO EAT LOBSTER?

Long associated with fine dining and decadent feasts, there was a time when a luxurious lobster dinner didn't exist. In fact, in Colonial-era America, these classy crustaceans were only fit to feed livestock and prisoners.

SURF SURPLUS

New England had a big problem in the 1600s—too much shellfish. It's documented that lobsters would wash up on the British colony's shores, piling up two feet high. What would be considered a gold rush today was seen as an off-putting abundance at the time, so much so that people would avoid eating them if possible, except in times of hardship. And it wasn't just foreign palates that were put off—Native Americans used them to bait their fishhooks to catch something else.

POOR MAN'S CHICKEN

The rich and respectable stopped eating lobster altogether, choosing instead to use the cheap protein to feed their livestock as well as their indentured servants. In one civil case in Massachusetts, some such servants successfully sued their boss, ensuring they could only be fed lobster a maximum of three times per week. This also meant it was the food of choice to keep prisoners alive, and the food of no choice for the poor.

It wasn't until late in the 19th century, when these same rich and respectable people started summering in Boston to escape New York and Washington, that lobster's stock began to rise. The tourists' taste for boiled lobster continued long after they returned home, demand for the crustacean skyrocketed, and prices soared.

64 DO MORE PEOPLE PREFER TEA OR COFFEE?

For some, choosing between tea and coffee is like choosing between your two best friends, but for many there's one clear winner, and that's often down to your country of residence. These beverages might not be the only way to start the day, but most countries tend to favor one or the other.

TRILLIONS OF TEA

Until the 18th century, coffee was mainly produced and enjoyed by African and Middle Eastern nations, while tea was popular in the Far East, but the rise of free trade in the 1800s soon changed that. In terms of production, retail sales, and the number of countries that favor it, coffee seems to dominate: 9.4 million tons of coffee is produced each year, which is double the amount of tea at 5.2 million tons. However, given that it only takes 0.07 ounce of tea to make a cup, versus 0.4 ounce of coffee, the world is actually producing coffee for a meager 850 billion cups a year, but enough tea for a whopping 2.35 trillion cups. That's 335 cups of tea a year for every single person—almost one a day.

LEGENDARY CUPPA

According to popular legend, tea came to be in around 2700 BC, when mythical ruler Shennong, the ancient Chinese "Father of Agriculture," took a nap under a camellia tree with a pot of boiling water to drink. Dried leaves from the tree floated into the water and stewed, creating the first ever pot of tea.

65 WHICH FOODS WILL BRING YOU GOOD LUCK?

Fancy munching a fatty sausage, chowing down on a bowl of beans, or slurping some soba noodles? Foodie superstitions from around the world are often focused on bringing prosperity and good fortune in the year ahead, so eat all three as you welcome in the New Year, and you might find it's your luckiest yet!

THIS LITTLE PIGGY . . .

A suckling pig is included in New Year's festivities in Spain, Cuba, Hungary, and Portugal, among other countries. Folklore claims that pigs are animals of progress— they always move forward when they're rooting around for food, and their high fat content symbolizes wealth and prosperity. Germans eat a variety of pork-based sausages throughout the holiday season, and their Austrian neighbors decorate the New Year dinner table with small pigs made from marzipan. But make sure you're not still eating Christmas turkey in the New Year—because these birds, as well as chickens, scratch backward, it's thought they could bring you setbacks and struggles in the months ahead.

BEAN THERE, DONE THAT

Beans in their seedlike form symbolize money, so many cultures cook up a bowl of legumes to welcome in the New Year in the hope some cash will come their way. In Brazil, the New Year is seen in with lentil soup or lentils and rice, while in the southern United States black-eyed peas (or cowpeas) are eaten in a dish called Hoppin' John, alongside leafy greens, which represent the country's paper money.

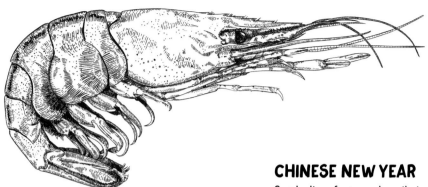

SOMETHING FISHY

If you're a fan of fish, you'll be pleased to hear that along with the many health benefits of eating seafood, there's also a lot of luck. Cod and other fish have been popular feast-time foods since the Middle Ages. Because they produce multiple eggs at a time, fish have long been considered a fertility symbol. In Japan you can pick up a *jubako*, a small food box filled with lucky foods for the New Year, which normally includes shrimp, herring roe, and sardines to bring you a long life, fertility, and bountiful crops.

SLURPEE SNACK

If you can control your New Year's hunger enough to eat a bowl of soba noodles delicately, you might just bag yourself a longer life. In Japan, China, and some other Asian nations, if you can eat a bowl of the long buckwheat noodles at New Year without breaking or chewing them, then a long life is coming your way. But make sure you're done slurping by midnight, otherwise it's considered bad luck.

CHINESE NEW YEAR

Symbolism features heavily in Chinese New Year—from the decorations to the gifts, but especially with the food. Foods whose names sound similar to words such as "gold," "luck," or "money" feature heavily. For example, tangerines and oranges are eaten in abundance— the word for "gold" sounds like "orange" and the word for "luck" sounds like "tangerine." Oranges with leaves are considered even luckier, because the greenery symbolizes longevity.

66 DOES DRINKING ALCOHOL WARM YOU UP?

There's nothing quite like a glass of something strong to help fight off the winter chill. But drinker, beware—while your skin may take on a rosy glow after a few alcoholic drinks, causing you to feel a rush of warmth, your core body temperature is actually dropping.

PERCEIVED WARMTH

Ethanol, the alcohol found in most booze, is a vasodilator. This means it has the effect of widening the blood vessels, in particular the capillaries just under the surface of your skin. More blood is able to pass through and the amount of blood under the skin's surface increases. This is why some people look flushed when they're drinking. You might feel warmer, too, because the increase in blood triggers heat-sensitive neurons in your skin that detect a rise in skin temperature.

This is fine if you're in a warm environment—the danger occurs when you go out in the cold. Normally, we feel the cold because our blood vessels have constricted and the blood has flowed away from our skin and into our internal organs to keep all the vital bits warm. With so much blood retained near the surface, rapidly cooling down, you might not feel the cold as much, but you'll be at a much higher risk of hypothermia.

SWEATS AND SHIVERS

Not only does alcohol lower your core body temperature, it also prevents your body's natural reflexes from kicking in to help warm you up. Normally, when your core temperature drops, you'll start to shiver—a natural reflex, caused by your skeletal muscles shaking to create warmth. But a study by the Army Research Institute of Environmental Medicine showed that alcohol stops you from shivering, so it's even harder to get your temperature back up. A 2005 study also showed that another reflex, sweating, was wrongly triggered by the increase in blood flow to the skin, which only serves to speed up the drop in core body temperature.

TOP ME UP

Drinking to excess might not warm you up, but you might experience a number of other interesting side effects.

DULL THE PAIN
Alcohol can dull your perception of pain, due to the dampening-down effect on the signals your sensory neurons pass to the brain. However, this can lessen over time, requiring you to drink more to achieve the same effect.

RELEASE THOSE INHIBITIONS
Alcohol can reduce inhibitory control in the cerebral cortex, the part of your brain that's associated with decision-making, social behavior, and information processing.

FEELING GOOD
While alcohol is actually responsible for increasing the production of stress hormones, such as corticosterone and corticotropin, it also increases the release of dopamine—the chemical that makes you feel great—so you keep going back for more.

YOU SNOOZE, YOU LOSE
Alcohol might make you sleepy, but if you've drunk a lot, the amount of slow-wave and REM sleep (i.e., good-quality sleep) you will have will be significantly reduced, as will your brain's ability to consolidate memories.

67 WHICH NUT CAN BLOW UP?

Delicious and nutritious, you wouldn't expect a batch of harmless nuts to be capable of causing some serious damage. But you'd be pistachio-so wrong.

UTTERLY NUTTERLY

If you're thinking of getting into the nut-shipping game, you might want to think again. Transporting pistachios around the world is a potentially lethal business. Those little green taste sensations need to be stored in strict conditions—on land or sea—to keep those around them safe. First off, they continue to absorb oxygen and release carbon dioxide, even after they've been harvested. A large quantity in an enclosed area with poor ventilation will suck all the breathable air out of the room, posing a serious suffocation risk.

NUT CRACKERS

But that's not the only thing to worry about. Temperature checking is vital too. Pistachios have a low water content and a high fat content. If there's too much humidity, then the nut's fat-cleaving enzymes start producing fatty acids. To break down these fats, the nut absorbs oxygen, spits out carbon dioxide, and loses water. This fat-burning process produces a lot of heat. If a large quantity is stored in a hot environment, this heat intensifies until the nuts catch fire, and sometimes even explode.

They're not the only food that has firework potential, or the only nut for that matter. Walnuts and cashews have been known to spontaneously combust on occasion, as have sunflower seeds, flax seeds, and apricot kernels.

QUIZ
FOOD AND DRINK

Stuffed full of tasty facts? Fill up your cup
and settle in for a foodie quiz session.

QUESTIONS:

1. Are you more or less at risk
   of hypothermia when you
   drink alcohol?

2. Which beverage has more cups
   produced every year—tea or
   coffee?

3. What was known as "poor man's
   chicken"?

4. In Roman times a *salarium* was a
   spa resort where soldiers went to
   relax after fighting—true or false?

5. What popular confection did
   Thomas Adams develop from his
   experiments with chicle resin?

6. In which country was
   machine-sliced bread invented?

7. The Scoville scale measures the
   heat of what: the sun, chilies, or
   the Sahara desert?

8. What is known as the "King of
   all Cheeses"?

9. Pistachios continue to absorb
   oxygen after they are harvested.
   True or false?

10. In many countries, which animal
    symbolizes progress because it
    always moves forward when eating?

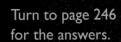

Turn to page 246
for the answers.

LITERATURE

68 WHAT WAS VICTOR HUGO'S CURE FOR WRITER'S BLOCK?

Ernest Hemingway said to stop when the going's good so you never get writer's block in the first place. But celebrated French author Victor Hugo had a different strategy altogether.

GENIUS IN THE BUFF

His literary works of genius include *Les Misérables*, but that didn't stop writer's block from creeping up on the Frenchman from time to time. When he was working on a book, Hugo would lock himself away in his study—pen and paper his only companions. When he got stuck, he would remove his clothes and instruct his servants to take them away and only return them to him when he had finished the day's writing. Stark naked, except for a huge gray shawl which he bought while writing *The Hunchback of Notre-Dame*, he had no option but to stay in the room and get on with it.

NAKED ESCAPADES

Nudity was probably a good motivator for Hugo, who was reportedly a big fan of the ladies, having hundreds of sexual partners in his lifetime. Despite being married to Adèle Foucher for 46 years—he claimed they had sex nine times the night they wed—Hugo continued to frequent Paris's many brothels. When he died at 83, the city's brothels closed down for a day of mourning to honor their best customer.

HUNGER STRIKES

Hugo's eccentricity didn't stop at naked writing—he threw lavish dinner parties for up to 30 guests every night. As the host with the most, he had a party trick to match. After stuffing a whole orange and as many sugar lumps as he could manage in his mouth, he'd swallow the lot washed down with two glasses of kirsch.

69 WHAT DID ROALD DAHL KNOW ABOUT CHOCOLATE?

They say authors should write about what they know. While Roald Dahl's stories were filled with unusual characters and fantastical scenarios, when it came to writing *Charlie and the Chocolate Factory* he was definitely harking back to his childhood, when he was a taster for one of the world's biggest chocolate factories.

BOARDING AND GORGING

Between 1930 and 1934, Dahl attended Repton, a boarding school in Derbyshire, England, where he and his classmates were guinea pigs for nearby Birmingham chocolatier Cadbury. Every now and then a cardboard box would arrive in the boardinghouse with 12 different chocolate bars, as Dahl explains in his autobiographical book *Boy*. The box also contained a piece of paper for the boys to note their score out of ten for each bar, and to make any comments. Dahl recalls that all the boys took their chocolate-testing responsibilities very seriously and that the experience opened his mind to the idea of inventing rooms in chocolate factories where new treats were dreamed up by men and women in white coats. Thirty-five years later, he would draw on those daydreams to create the world of Willy Wonka's extraordinary factory.

THE IMPORTANCE OF CHOCOLATE

Dahl loved chocolate so much, he dedicated an entire chapter to it in *The Roald Dahl Cookbook*, where he wrote his "History of Chocolate," spanning the seven years (1930–37) when his favorite chocolate bars were released. He once told a group of schoolchildren that they shouldn't bother remembering the kings and queens, just these dates.

70 CAN MUGGLES PLAY QUIDDITCH?

Even if you've never read J.K. Rowling's *Harry Potter* books or seen the film adaptations, you've still probably heard of quidditch, the broomstick-brandishing sport that forms an integral part of her wizarding world.

NOT JUST FOR WIZARDS

In Rowling's novels, it's a sport that's been played for nearly 1,000 years by the magical folk who, unbeknown to us, exist alongside us "muggles," or regular non-magic humans. It's a seven-a-side aerial game that features four balls—a Quaffle, two Bludgers, and a Golden Snitch. Each team has three goal hoops at each end of the arena, and the aim of the game is to score the most points by throwing the Quaffle through these goal hoops. The game ends when the Golden Snitch—a smaller ball with wings—is caught by either team. You'll never see a muggle chasing a Golden Snitch in Rowling's fictional world, but a real-life quidditch phenomenon has swept the world, and you don't even have to be a *Harry Potter* fan to play.

THE REAL-LIFE RULES

To all intents and purposes, real-life quidditch is very similar to its magic counterpart. In this mixed-gender contact sport, two teams of seven are pitted against each other. According to the International Quidditch Association, players must wear colored headbands to identify themselves as either the keeper, who guards the hoops at each end of the field where points are scored; the seeker, who must chase the "snitch runner"; a chaser, who scores goals by throwing or kicking a volleyball through the hoops; or a beater, who must prevent the other team from scoring points by throwing dodge balls at them.

MAKING MAGIC AROUND THE WORLD

The real-life International Quidditch Association serves some 20 national governing bodies across six continents. Just like in the book, quidditch has its own world cup, which has taken place every two years since 2012. The 2018 IQA World Cup was held in Florence, Italy, and 29 teams competed, including Slovenia, Brazil, and South Korea; the United States won the tournament.

FIVE QUICK FACTS

1 THE VERY HUNGRY CATERPILLAR WAS ALMOST A WORM

An early draft of Eric Carle's 1969 children's classic featured a worm as the titular insatiable character, but an editor made the suggestion that it should be a caterpillar instead.

2 JACK KEROUAC NEVER LEARNED TO DRIVE

Despite his most well-known novel, *On the Road*, being based on the author's own road trips across the United States, the Beat Generation legend never got behind the wheel himself.

3 PETER PAN WAS ORIGINALLY A VILLAIN

J.M. Barrie's much-loved book was originally a play, with Peter as the story's troublemaker. But the theatrical team needed time to switch the sets, so Barrie introduced a scene with a pirate ship to buy them time, and Captain Hook was born.

4 JAMES JOYCE LEFT IRELAND AS SOON AS HE COULD

The author was famous for writing about his homeland, Dublin in particular, but spent most of his adult life living elsewhere, in Trieste, Paris, and Zurich. He didn't even go back for his father's funeral.

5 TONI MORRISON WORKED AS AN EDITOR FOR 20 YEARS

The Nobel Prize–winning author was the first black editor at Random House—a post she took after teaching English at universities. There she helped publish books by celebrated black authors, including Toni Cade Bambara, Gayl Jones, Angela Davis, and Muhammad Ali.

71 WHY DID THE FBI HAVE A FILE ON ERNEST HEMINGWAY?

In 1983, after a Freedom of Information petition by a University of Colorado academic who was working on a biography, the FBI released a 122-page file on American author and journalist Ernest Hemingway. The documents it contained spanned the years 1942 to 1974, despite the fact that Hemingway died in 1961.

INTELLIGENT OPERATIVE

Between 1942 and 1944, Hemingway undertook intelligence work in Havana, Cuba, where he lived with his third wife, Martha. His activities were encouraged by Spruille Braden, the United States ambassador to Cuba, and he set up what he dubbed the "crook factory" to keep tabs on the Spanish immigrants who supported the dictator Francisco Franco and supported the German–Italian Axis. He was given $1,000 per month to pay his network of 26 informants.

LIFE BEFORE LITERATURE

Despite dying at 61, Hemingway packed a lot into his life. Even before he'd published any of his novels, he'd already worked as a cub reporter for a Kansas City newspaper straight out of high school, and as a member of the volunteer ambulance unit in the Italian army during World War I. After the war, he worked as a reporter for both American and Canadian newspapers, covering events in Europe. In the 1920s, he worked as a correspondent in Paris, socializing with a group of international artists that included F. Scott Fitzgerald, Pablo Picasso, and James Joyce.

Meanwhile, the FBI director, J. Edgar Hoover, ordered that Hemingway be put under surveillance. Hoover and others in the intelligence community believed Hemingway had ties to the Communist Party and that his intelligence information was not credible. The crook factory was dissolved in 1943, but the author continued to embark on submarine-hunting trips on his fishing boat for about two years. And the Hemingway file reveals that, even decades later, reports were filed about him and his phones were tapped.

THE TOLL OF SURVEILLANCE

On July 1, 1961, at his home in Ketchum, Idaho, Ernest Hemingway drew his favorite shotgun from his gun rack and, while his fourth wife, Mary, slept upstairs, ended his own life. His final year had been riddled with paranoia and depression. Friends of Hemingway have talked since about his belief that the FBI was keeping him under surveillance. He was also deeply anxious about his latest manuscript, a memoir about Paris, which would be published posthumously as *A Moveable Feast*. Seven

months before his death, he was checked into the psychiatric wing of a Minnesota hospital, where he received electric shock treatments. During a release from the ward, he twice tried to kill himself, and while on a flight he tried to jump from the plane. All the while he believed the phones were bugged and the FBI was watching him.

One of the most recent reports in the file is dated January 13, 1961. Addressed to Hoover, it recounts how Hemingway was at that time a patient at the Mayo Clinc and that he was "seriously ill, both physically and mentally."

72 WHO INVENTED THE BRA CLASP?

On December 19, 1871, Samuel L. Clemens was granted a patent for "adjustable and detachable elastic straps for vests, pantaloons, or other garments requiring straps." An illustration supplied with the application shows the inventor had devised an ingenious elasticated clasp, later to become a universal feature of bras. So who was this canny inventor?

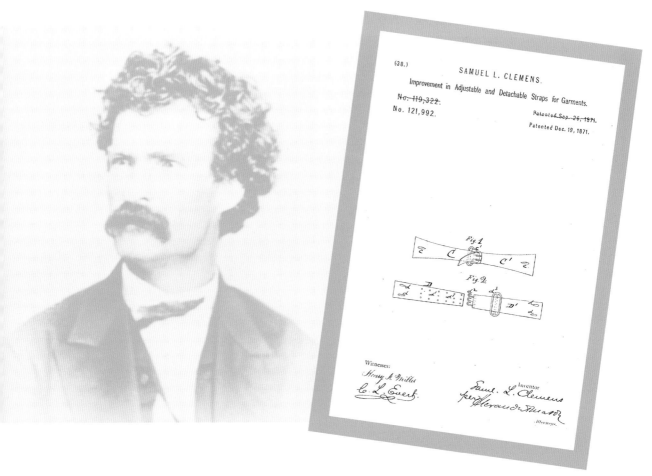

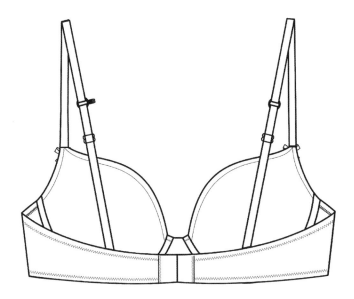

INVENTING SUCCESS

The device was a success and was used for shirts, underpants, and women's corsets. Twain had hoped that his new invention would bring about the death of suspenders, which he found most uncomfortable. At the time, belts were largely decorative, so this elastic fastener provided people with another option for keeping their clothes in place. The "bra clasp" was not Twain's only invention. He received two more patents—one, less successful, for a history trivia game that never went into production, and the second for an "improvement in scrap books." As a scrapbook enthusiast, Twain hoped to do away with the gluing element of the hobby with his self-pasting idea. The pages of the book would be entirely covered "on one or both sides" with what Twain described as "mucilage or other suitable adhesive substance." It would only be necessary to moisten the part of the page you wanted to stick something to. The invention was a success and sold 25,000 copies.

THE INVENTIONS OF MARK TWAIN

Samuel L. Clemens was Mark Twain's given name. While his most famous works—*The Adventures of Tom Sawyer* and *Adventures of Huckleberry Finn*—have become classics of American literature, his adjustable clasp has had a huge impact on the comfort and fit of women's lingerie for over 150 years. The patent also shows that Twain wanted the strap to be a flexible addition to clothing that could be attached and detached between different garments, to hold together any ill-fitting piece of clothing. "When changing garments the strap may readily be detached from one and put on another," he wrote. "The advantages of such an adjustable and detachable elastic strap are so obvious that they need no explanation."

BETTING ON TYPE

Sadly, when it came to getting on board with other people's ideas, Twain was not so fortunate. He lost the majority of his wealth after buying the rights to a typesetting machine. The investment cost him what would be $8 million in today's money. He believed the machine would become the future of print but, mired with problems, it was soon overtaken by the Linotype typecasting machine, leaving Twain with serious financial problems.

73 WHAT DID VLADIMIR NABOKOV KEEP IN HIS CABINET?

Russian-American novelist Nabokov is internationally renowned for his famous novels, most notably the 1955 work *Lolita*—but he was also a distinguished entomologist. The pinnacle of this work is the "Nabokov Genitalia Cabinet," containing hundreds of documents and cigar boxes filled with butterfly penises.

WINGS AND THINGS

Nabokov's passion for insects, especially butterflies, began from a young age, and developed into a serious study of lepidoptera when he enrolled at Cambridge University. Twenty years later, after completing ten novels, he emigrated to New York and soon began a six-year stint at Harvard, where he spent 14-hour days studying butterflies. At first his research led him to believe that a butterfly's key identifying feature was its wing pattern, but later he came to theorize that butterfly genitalia, visible only under a microscope, were more revealing of their evolutionary journey. As a result, he recorded and illustrated hundreds of these intricate anatomical structures and stored them methodically in a small wooden cabinet, now held in the Entomology Department of Harvard's Museum of Comparative Zoology.

REWRITING SCIENCE

During his lifetime, Nabokov's lepidopterology theories were not taken seriously—specifically, his belief that a particular genus of *Polyommatus*, the blues, had originated in Asia and traveled through Siberia and then south as far as Chile. Since his death in 1977, more attention has been paid to his work, and gene-sequencing technology has proved a number of his theories to be true. His professional work in the field ended after his time at Harvard, but he never stopped catching butterflies for his collection.

74 WHAT IS THE SLOWEST-SELLING BOOK OF ALL TIME?

Some books don't sell many copies at all, but after it's clear no one wants them, they are soon found to be out of print. But one author's unwanted books were sitting around waiting for a buyer for nearly 200 years.

IT'S ALL LATIN TO ME

The slowest-selling book of all time is probably David Wilkins's translation of the Bible's New Testament, according to Guinness World Records. Published in 1716 by Oxford University Press and titled *Novum Testamentum Aegyptium*, it was based on Coptic manuscripts held at Oxford's Bodleian library, which he translated into Latin. Unusually for an Oxford author, Wilkins hadn't studied or worked at Oxford University—the esteemed institution refused him an MA four years earlier. The book was criticized by other scholars, but that didn't stop 500 copies from being printed. Unfortunately, it might have stopped them from being snapped up. It would take 191 years for the last copy to sell in 1907, which means people bought the book, but only at a rate of one every 20 weeks.

HOLY MOLEY!

Bizarrely, Wilkins was on the right lines in terms of subject matter. The best-selling book of all time is the Bible. Exact figures are impossible to calculate, but the Bible Society estimates that 2.5 billion copies were printed between 1815 and 1975. It's likely the figure now surpasses 5 billion. Coming in a close second in a much shorter time span is *Quotations from the Works of Mao Zedong (Tse-tung)*. Between 1966 and 1971 it was mandatory to have a copy in China, resulting in 800 million copies being sold or distributed.

75 WHAT HAPPENED TO THE REAL WINNIE-THE-POOH?

Winnie-the-Pooh, by A.A. Milne, was first published in 1926. With translations in 50 languages, including Czech, Afrikaans, and Esperanto, sales of Pooh titles now exceed 50 million globally. But the honey-loving Pooh was inspired by a real-life black bear that most people know nothing about.

BOUGHT BEAR, $20

On August 24, 1914, Harry Colebourn, a captain in the Canadian Army, made a rather unusual note in his diary: "Left Port Arthur, 7 am, On train, bought bear, $20." Colebourn, a veterinary surgeon, was part of the Canadian Army Veterinarian Corps on his way to the World War I battlefields. His mission: to look after the horses in the cavalry units. It comes as no surprise that this animal lover felt compelled to purchase the orphaned black bear cub, whose mother had been killed by a trapper in White River, Ontario. He named her Winnipeg, shortened to "Winnie," after his hometown.

WINNIE THE ARMY BEAR

At the start of the war, Captain Colebourn's regiment traveled to Europe, encamping at the Salisbury Plain training ground in Wiltshire, England. Winnie came along as a mascot and lived there with the soldiers for four months—she kept everyone entertained and was reportedly an excellent navigator. Unfortunately, this unlikely friendship was not to last. Knowing that his regiment would soon be sent to the front line in France, on December 9, 1914, Colebourn borrowed a car and drove Winnie to London Zoo. He asked the zoo to take care of her until he returned, but she soon settled in and became a star attraction for over 20 years.

WHEN SHE WAS VERY OLD

Winnipeg died of old age in May 1934, but her legacy lives on at London's Royal College of Surgeons' Hunterian Museum. Her skull was originally donated to a dental surgeon, who was the first to report on dental diseases in bears. He noted Winnie's loss of teeth, which he believed was caused by her old age and her food habits—it's believed Christopher Robin did in fact feed her honey and other treats. More recently, examinations have revealed that she suffered from chronic periodontitis—an inflammation or loss of connective tissues surrounding or supporting the teeth. Winnie's skull, along with those of other animals, has provided invaluable evidence to help zoo vets treat animals living in captivity.

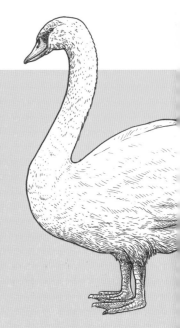

A NEW FRIEND

Winnie's true star power, however, was still to emerge. Due to her friendly nature, she was trusted entirely by the zookeepers; they even let children go inside her enclosure, ride on her back, and hand-feed her treats. As a result, she was beloved by children, none more so than a little boy named Christopher Robin, A.A. Milne's son. The father and son were frequent visitors to the zoo, and soon Christopher Robin had renamed his stuffed bear Winnie in honor of his new friend. While his father couldn't bring the real-life bear home, he combined her name with that of Christopher Robin's pet swan, "Pooh," to create the name of a bear generations of children have enjoyed since.

76 WHICH WRITER WAS THE 19TH CENTURY'S MOST PHOTOGRAPHED AMERICAN?

Born into slavery in 1818, abolitionist, author, and presidential advisor Frederick Douglass escaped to freedom and then worked tirelessly to help others get theirs. One of the tricks he had up his sleeve was the old-fashioned version of the selfie.

IMAGE IS EVERYTHING

Throughout his life, Douglass sat for nearly 160 photographic portraits—more than Abraham Lincoln. What Douglass recognized early on, and ahead of his time, was the power of the photo to communicate, challenge, and transform people's perceptions, in this case about black people. The racist slave-owner mentality was propagated on the idea that black people were physically and mentally inferior to whites. White ethnologists who traveled around the world used photography to record and disseminate information about anatomical differences, and these dehumanizing photographs were in stark contrast to the ones of Frederick Douglass.

POWER POSE

Douglass was always shown smartly dressed in a suit and tie, with a serious and determined expression, without the props or costumes often associated with portraits of non-European ethnicities. Despite being wary of photographers' manipulations, he made sure his portraits reflected his own power and sought to help others reclaim theirs. At a time when photography was becoming more widely available—many small towns had a photographic studio and traveling photographers would set up shop to take people's portraits—Douglass encouraged others to follow his lead. "Men of all conditions may see themselves as others see them," he said in an 1861 lecture titled *Pictures and Progress*. "What was once the exclusive luxury of the rich and great is now within reach of all."

77 WHY DID JAPANESE AUTHOR HARUKI MURAKAMI START OUT WRITING IN ENGLISH?

As one of the most internationally recognized Japanese authors, he has had his work translated into over 50 languages, but when Murakami started out, he tried writing in English first.

PLAYING HARDBALL

Before he wrote his first novel, Japanese literary great Murakami was making ends meet and running a jazz club with his wife in Tokyo. Then, while he sat in Jingu Stadium watching a baseball game, he had an epiphany—perhaps he could write a novel. That night he started writing, and *Hear the Wind Sing* was the result. For over 10 months he worked on the book, and it wasn't without its challenges. To try to find his own unique style that would set him apart from other Japanese writers, he wrote the first chapter in English. With limited vocabulary and the ability to write only in short, simple sentences, the result was what he described as "a rough, uncultivated kind of prose." But the exercise did the trick and he was able to complete the novel in Japanese. It would be the first of many.

AGONY UNCLE

The celebrated author of *The Wind-Up Bird Chronicle* is somewhat of a rare bird himself, rarely giving interviews or making public appearances. That's not to say that he hasn't interacted with his fans. In 2015 he wrote an advice column called "Mr. Murakami's Place," where he responded to readers' questions. Over the month that the column ran for, he received more than 37,000 queries from all over the world and managed to respond to 3,716 of them. He also started a radio show in Japan called *Murakami Radio: Run & Songs.*

78 HOW MANY LANGUAGES DID J. R. R. TOLKIEN INVENT?

J.R.R. Tolkien's famous novels—*The Hobbit* and *The Lord of the Rings*, published between 1937 and 1955— have brought joy to generations of readers. Both stories are set in the imaginative world of Middle-earth. Its mythology is expansive and detailed, made apparent through Tolkien's use of language.

SCHOLARLY ENDEAVORS

John Ronald Reuel Tolkien's love for language was instilled early on by his mother, who taught him Latin, French, and German at home. In a 1968 interview with the *Telegraph*, Tolkien said: "When I was supposed to be studying Latin and Greek, I studied Welsh and English. When I was supposed to be concentrating on English, I took up Finnish."

He helped create the nonsense childhood languages Animalic and Nevbosh with friends, and later created his own called Naffarin, based on Latin and Spanish. But it was Tolkien's study of Welsh—he would go on to teach medieval Welsh at the University of Leeds for five years—and later Finnish that helped him to develop the mystical languages in *The Lord of the Rings*.

LOST IN TRANSLATION

None of Tolkien's languages were ever finished to the point where they could be used to fully communicate today, and some were only mentioned in the books but not spoken. There was also Dwarvish (known as Khuzdul), Entish, and Black Speech, spoken by the servants of Sauron, including the Orcs. The latter is the language in which the famous "One Ring to rule them all . . ." inscription is written. Middle-earth also features a number of "Mannish" languages and dialects spoken by Men. Westron is the most commonly spoken language of Men, which is also spoken by Hobbits, and is "translated" into English throughout the books for the reader. It's possible that, taking into consideration his Middle-earth work and earlier experimentation with linguistics, Tolkien invented over 20 new languages in his lifetime.

HOW TO SPEAK ELF

Rather than the languages being part of the stories, Tolkien saw the stories and world he created as a place for these languages, and the mythology surrounding them, to exist. In Ruth S. Noel's book *The Languages of Tolkien's Middle-earth*, she identifies 14 languages thought up by the author. But the two most developed Middle-earth languages are Quenya and Sindarin. Also known as High-Elven and Grey-Elven, these two Elvish languages have close ties to Finnish and Welsh, respectively, and their own historical language roots and dialects.

By the time the first two books in the *Lord of the Rings* trilogy were published in 1954, Tolkien had been developing these languages for 40 years. Quenya, which developed out of an earlier language called Qenya, is the Elvish version of Latin—it's a literary language used for poetry, song, and magic. Sindarin, on the other hand, is the more commonly "spoken" language, used by the Elves in his books to communicate. Tolkien's languages developed over time, even after the publication of the three *Lord of the Rings* novels. He made various changes to the Elvish texts in the second and revised editions.

79 WHAT IS THE LONGEST BOOK EVER WRITTEN?

Like the old adage "How long is a piece of string?" the answer to this lengthy question is debatable. Some argue that a book's length should be measured in words; others say characters or even pages. But the Guinness World Record for the longest novel has stood for many years.

TIME TO READ

The title holder is *À la recherche du temps perdu*, or *In Search of Lost Time*, by Marcel Proust, which was published in a series of 13 volumes from 1913 to 1927. The novel contains an estimated 1.3 million words and 9,609,000 characters (including spaces). However, there are other claimants to the title. On word count alone, Madeleine and George de Scudéry's *Artamène ou le Grand Cyrus* (1649–53), a ten-volume romantic epic containing an estimated 2.1 million words, is clearly a front-runner, while there are fan fiction stories online that run to well over 3 million words.

A PAPER TRAIL

While the debate rages on, there's one manuscript that is a strong contender for longest physical book. A draft of Jack Kerouac's *On the Road*, now considered a 20th-century classic, was typed out by the author on a roll of paper that he'd taped together from 12-foot reams. The reason? So he could type continuously without being interrupted. The result was a 120-foot manuscript. In 2001, Jim Irsay, owner of the Indianapolis Colts, paid $2.43 million for the scroll and loaned it to the Lilly Library at Indiana University.

QUIZ
LITERATURE

Literally stuffed full of facts? See how much of that bookish knowledge you've absorbed with this little quiz.

QUESTIONS:

1. What did Victor Hugo use to keep warm while he wrote with no clothes on?

2. Which chocolate manufacturer sent taste tests to Roald Dahl's boarding school—Hershey's or Cadbury?

3. The Golden Snitch appears in which popular book series about a boy wizard?

4. Who invented the elastic clasp most famously used for bras?

5. Which language was not invented by J.R.R. Tolkien—Quenya, Sindarin, or Klingon?

6. What did Ernest Hemingway do while he was in Cuba?

7. Vladimir Nabokov studied lepidoptera, otherwise known as which winged insect?

8. Was David Wilkins's Bible published by Oxford University Press or Cambridge University Press?

9. Haruki Murakami has written an agony uncle column. True or false?

10. Winnie-the-Pooh was a real bear—true or false?

Turn to page 247 for the answers.

GEOGRAPHY

80 HOW CLOSE HAVE WE GOTTEN TO THE CENTER OF THE EARTH?

The center of the Earth is not a very hospitable place. At around 3,958 miles below the Earth's surface, the pressure is 3.6 million atmospheres—that's the same as having 47,700 elephants sitting on your head. It's no wonder we've literally barely scratched the surface when it comes to subterranean exploration.

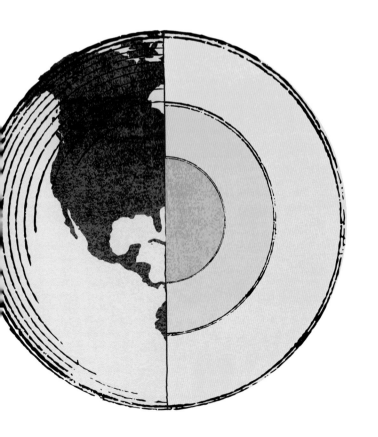

HEATING UP

The Earth is made up of a number of layers, which become increasingly hot the closer you get to the center. The outer shell, known as the crust, is about 30 miles thick, and for every 0.6 mile you travel toward the Earth's center, the temperature increases by 77°F. To put that depth into perspective, one mile is the average depth of the Grand Canyon or the bottom of Russia's Lake Baikal. Beneath the crust is the upper mantle, made up of partially molten rock, where temperatures are believed to range from 1,200°F to 2,200°F. Under the mantle and the outer core lies the inner core, which scientists believe has a temperature of 10,300°F—roughly the same temperature as the sun's photosphere.

JOURNEY TO THE BOTTOM OF THE OCEAN

The deepest artificial hole is only marginally closer to the center of the Earth than the deepest part of the ocean. That's Challenger Deep at the bottom of the Mariana Trench in the Pacific. More people have been to the Moon than to this point on our own planet. In 2012, film producer James Cameron became the third person ever to reach the bottom of this 36,062-foot-deep cavern, in a submarine called *Deepsea Challenger*. He spent three hours exploring the ocean bed and described it as "quite a sterile, almost desert-like space."

HOLEY MOLEY!

These extreme temperatures mean that we've made few inroads into the Earth's crust. Drilling is the obvious method to get down there, but the extreme temperatures, combined with the friction created by the drill bit driving through the rock, mean that conventional drill-bit materials become unviable at a certain depth. The deepest artificial hole drilled by humans is the Kola Superdeep Borehole in Russia. Starting in 1970, engineers spent 19 years drilling and made it just 7.62 miles below the Earth's surface—not even a quarter of the way to the crust. And technically we've never made it this far, just our machines. In second place is Mponeng Gold Mine, South Africa, where miners travel a distance of up to 2.42 miles below the surface. Eight of the deepest mines in the world are situated in South Africa.

In 2015, one ongoing exploratory expedition attempted to use the Indian Ocean's depths to drill down to the Earth's mantle—a challenge attempted a few times but never achieved. They were aiming to target the Moho border, where the crust and mantle meet, to extract "gabbros"—rocks created when slow-cooling magma is caught under the surface of the crust-mantle transition. Unfortunately, after nearly two months at sea, the researchers and crew of the *JOIDES* (Joint Oceanographic Institutions for Deep Sampling) *Resolution* returned to dry land after falling short of their planned 4,265-foot hole by 1,676 feet.

81 HOW DO YOU GET TO THE BERMUDA TRIANGLE?

The Bermuda Triangle, or Devil's Triangle, is a roughly 500,000-square-mile area of the Atlantic Ocean between Bermuda, San Juan in Puerto Rico, and Miami, Florida. The name was coined in a 1964 magazine article after a number of mysterious disappearances and inexplicable activity made the region a hot topic for conspiracy theorists.

THE OFFICIAL LINE

In a sense, there's no way to "get" to the Bermuda Triangle because technically it doesn't exist. The U.S. Board on Geographic Names does not recognize the Bermuda Triangle as an official name, and no file is maintained on the area. Both the U.S. Navy and U.S. Coast Guard claim that there are no supernatural forces at work. As yet, there is no hard evidence to prove that disappearances occur at a significantly higher rates in this part of the ocean than any other well-traversed area. The Coast Guard's official line is: "In a review of many aircraft and vessel losses in the area over the years ... No extraordinary factors have ever been identified."

GOING, GOING, GONE!

Many mysterious disappearances over the years have led to the theories surrounding the Bermuda Triangle. There was the 1920 disappearance of 11 crew members from aboard the Carroll A. Deering; then there were the five U.S. Navy planes that took off from Fort Lauderdale in 1945, never to be heard from or seen again; and then the 1948 vanishing of Captain Robert Lindquist and his plane off the Miami coast. The bizarre disappearances of the crew from the Carroll A. Deering and the many other vessels and planes that have gone missing over the years have added fuel to the theorizing fire. Some believe that extraterrestrials abduct humans from the region, while others believe a vortex is sucking these crew members into another dimension. There's also the theory that energy crystals from the lost city of Atlantis, which some believe sank here, are controlling the ships and planes above. But the more pragmatic types think most of these mysteries can be explained by science.

Bermuda

Atlantic Ocean

Caribbean Sea

FIVE QUICK FACTS

1 **AFRICA IS THE ONLY CONTINENT IN ALL FOUR HEMISPHERES**

Its global position means parts of Africa fall in the north, south, east, and west hemispheres. It's also the only continent that has land on the equator and the prime meridian.

2 **POINT NEMO IS REALLY HARD TO GET TO**

Also known as the Pole of Inaccessibility, this spot in the Pacific Ocean is located 1,670 miles away from land. Sometimes, the nearest humans are astronauts orbiting on the International Space Station when it's positioned 258 miles skywards.

3 **AUSTRALIA IS HOME TO THE WORLD'S LONGEST FENCE**

The Dingo Fence, first built in the 1880s, is designed to stop wild dogs from helping themselves to farmers' sheep. It spans 3,488 miles of Australia's southeastern desert.

4 **ICELAND IS GROWING**

With only 360,000 residents, Iceland is a small country, but it's getting bigger. Due to the movement of the North American and European tectonic plates, it's growing by 2 inches every year.

5 **THERE ARE TWO NEIGHBORING ISLANDS THAT ARE NEARLY A DAY APART**

The Diomede Islands, nicknamed Tomorrow and Yesterday Island, are situated just 2.4 miles apart, but because one is Russian and the other is American, they're in different time zones and have a 21-hour time difference.

82 WHICH POINT ON EARTH IS CLOSEST TO SPACE?

The peak of Mount Everest might be the top of the tallest mountain on Earth, but there are a number of other places you could stand if you wanted to be closer to space. Ecuador's Mount Chimborazo is the closest.

IMPRESSIVE PEAKS

Everest holds its title because mountains are traditionally compared based on their height above sea level. So while Chimborazo rises 3.8 miles above sea level, Everest pulls in a whopping 5.5 miles. However, the inactive Andean volcano is the world's highest peak if you measure mountains from the center of the Earth. On this basis, the peak of Chimborazo rises higher than any other mountain, at 3,977 miles—that's 1.2 miles farther from the center of the Earth than Everest.

SHAPING UP

So why the difference? It's all down to the shape of the planet. Earth is not a perfect sphere; it's slightly inflated around the middle—where equatorial countries are situated. Everest is located at 28 degrees north latitude, much closer to the North Pole, where the sphere flattens. Because the Earth's radius is about 13 miles wider at the equator, mountain peaks in countries like Ecuador and Kenya technically reach farther into space than their more earthly rivals, and Chimborazo is closest of all to the stars.

For those who like the idea of being on the top of the world but can't be fussed with all those weeks of training, hiking, and acclimatizing to scale Everest, reaching the top of Chimborazo is a much more achievable ambition—typically a one- or two-day hike after acclimatization.

83 WHERE CAN YOU FIND AN ISLAND IN A LAKE ON AN ISLAND IN A LAKE ON AN ISLAND?

Map enthusiasts used to think that the world's largest sub-sub-sub-island was in a crater lake on Volcano Island in Lake Taal on the Philippine island of Luzon. But they were wrong . . .

AN ISLAND OF CURIOSITY

In 2014, the operational land imager on *Landsat 8* captured a satellite photo that found a larger one. The narrow island, which measures a fifth of a mile long and covers an area of about four acres, is found inside a lake, which is on an island, inside a lake, on Canada's Victoria Island, which is separated from the country's frozen tundra by the Coronation Gulf. Nameless and likely never visited by humans, the vast Victoria Island is the eighth-largest island in the world but is home to just 2,000 people—it's possible that it will be dethroned in time. The Canadian Arctic Archipelago is made up of 36,000 islands, and millions of lakes, ponds, and streams— that's a lot of looking at islands in lakes in islands in lakes in islands . . .

ISLANDS IN THE STREAM

This little island isn't Canada's only record holder. The nation is home to the world's largest island in a lake—Manitoulin Island in Lake Huron—and the world's largest lake on an island, which is Nettilling Lake on Baffin Island. If you fancy more tropical climes, you could visit the largest island in a lake on an island, which is Samosir—a volcanic isle smack in the middle of Lake Toba on the Indonesian island of Sumatra.

84 HOW MUCH WATER FLOWS OUT OF THE AMAZON RIVER?

The Amazon River might dispute its title for world's longest river with the Nile, but there's no denying its position when it comes to its water flow. At a staggering 286,440 cubic yards per second, the average discharge from this mighty South American behemoth is shoulders above the competition.

WILD RIVER

To put this in perspective, every second of every day the volume of nearly 90 Olympic-sized swimming pools is gushing out of the Amazon's mouth—an estimated one-sixth of the world's rivers' discharge. And this is an impressive mouth. Where the river meets the Atlantic Ocean in eastern Brazil, its delta is 200 miles wide and features the world's largest freshwater island, Marajó, which is roughly the size of Switzerland.

RAINY DAYS

Where does all that water come from? A network of approximately 1,100 tributaries, which carry water a distance of over 4,100 miles, span an area of around 2.7 million square miles. The country of India covers only 1.3 million square miles. The vast quantities of water are thanks to the torrential rainfall the huge Amazon basin receives—between 60 and 120 inches per year, depending on the location. The rain is thanks in part to eastern trade winds blowing in off the Atlantic and also the vegetation that makes up the Amazon's biome. Water is soaked up through the soil by plants, evaporates, and falls as rain back into the basin. And as the weather changes, so does the river. Parts that can measure $1\frac{1}{2}$ or 2 miles across when it's dry can become 30-mile chasms in the wet season, with river speeds of up to $4\frac{1}{2}$ miles per hour.

WEST MEETS EAST

The mighty river starts high up in the Peruvian Andes and makes its way east. But the source is a mere 120 miles from where the river used to end. Millions of years ago, the river emptied into the Pacific instead, but the collision of the South American and Nazca tectonic plates brought about the creation of the Andes mountain range about 65 million years ago. Eventually this blocked the flow of the river, creating freshwater lakes and gradually reversing the river's flow. It's estimated that the river reached the Atlantic Ocean about 10 million years ago.

SOMETHING FISHY

With all that water, it's no surprise that the Amazon is home to an astonishing array of life. It's estimated that over 2,500 different fish species are living in the river—more than the entire Atlantic Ocean—with some experts believing the number could be significantly higher. The biodiversity of the region has led to catfish weighing over 200 pounds, 15-foot-long arapaima, and the parasitic candiru—a tiny fish that has been known to swim up the urethra of people who urinate in the river. And if that's not terrifying enough, bull sharks, which have the ability to adapt from their usual saltwater habitat to that of the river, have been found as far as 2,500 miles upstream from the sea.

85 WHO OWNS ANTARCTICA?

On December 1, 1959, 12 countries entered into the Antarctic Treaty, stating that all parties "[recognize] that it is in the interest of all mankind that Antarctica shall continue forever to be used exclusively for peaceful purposes and shall not become the scene or object of international discord."

ICY CLAIMS

Of the 12 signatory countries, all of which had had scientists active in Antarctica between 1957 and 1958, seven—Argentina, Australia, Chile, France, New Zealand, Norway, and the United Kingdom—had existing territorial claims to parts of the continent. While the treaty states that nobody holds ownership of any land on Antarctica, it technically protects those claims and prohibits further claims from being made. One large segment of Antarctica was not claimed at the time of the treaty and remains the largest segment of unclaimed land on Earth.

IN AGREEMENT

Since the original 12 nations signed the treaty, 41 other countries have signed up to the same agreement. Among other things, they're committed to carrying out their work peacefully and cooperatively, with no military presence, and to sharing any scientific observations and results made from Antarctica with the other nations. No nuclear explosions or mining are permitted. The future importance of Antarctica is plain to see—it's believed to hold significant oil reserves, and has 70 percent of the world's freshwater supply.

86 HOW HIGH UP CAN HUMANS LIVE?

The peak elevation for permanent human residence is widely considered to be 17,000 feet. Above this altitude, life would be a struggle. Altitude sickness, which can affect people from 10,000 feet, can cause oxygen deficiency (which damages cells) and a deadly buildup of fluid in the lungs and brain.

GOING FOR GOLD

The world's highest city lies in the Peruvian Andes, on the side of Mount Ananea. With a population of some 50,000, La Rinconada sits beside a giant glacier, at a height of 16,700 feet. Despite the fact that the city lacks amenities and temperatures are subzero most of the year, the population has soared in recent years due to a gold-mining operation located several days' walk away along a precarious road. The mines are largely unregulated and run illegally, and miners are paid by an ancient system known as *cachorreo*—they work unpaid for 30 days but can keep any gold they find on the last day of the month. Every day, they face perilous working conditions and high levels of mercury and cyanide.

GREAT ADAPTATIONS

Research has shown that communities that live at such high altitudes for significant periods, such as the Himalayan Sherpas, develop genetic adaptations to cope with the extreme conditions, such as compactly built bodies with adapted hearts and lungs. But it's unlikely the residents of La Rinconada would want to live much higher up, even if their bodies could handle it, because it would be impossible to grow crops or keep livestock.

87 WHY CAN YOU GET AWAY WITH MURDER IN YELLOWSTONE NATIONAL PARK?

While it's never wise to get into the habit of murdering people, there's one place in the United States where a legal loophole means you could do it with impunity.

NOT-SO-MELLOW YELLOWSTONE

If you were dead-set on taking out your enemies, it might be worth considering a quick trip, enemies in tow, to a 50-square-mile area of land in Yellowstone National Park. It's known as a "zone of death" for the legal conundrum it's created. When the park was founded in 1872, the states of Montana, Wyoming, and Idaho were yet to join the Union. By 1890 they had joined, with most of the park falling inside the Wyoming border and a small part of it in Montana. Another small parcel of the park was part of Idaho.

Years later, in 2005, Brian Kalt, a law professor at Michigan State University College of Law, published a paper about the region. He titled it *The Perfect Crime*, and here's why. The district court that presides over crimes committed in all of Yellowstone is in the state of Wyoming. That means that unlike any other district in the United States, the District of Wyoming includes land in other states. If you committed a serious crime in the Idaho part of the park, you'd still be taken to Wyoming to be tried in court. However, the Sixth Amendment to the U.S. Constitution says:

"In all criminal prosecutions, the accused shall enjoy the right to a speedy and public trial, by an impartial jury of the State and district wherein the crime shall have been committed . . ."

LETTER OF THE LAW

That means that you could invoke your constitutional right to be tried back in Idaho, where you committed the crime. But because the law insists that the jury must be made up of jurors from the state and district where the crime was committed, the juror pool must include people who live both in the state of Idaho and in the District of Wyoming—in other words, in the part of the park where you committed the crime. Problem is, absolutely no one lives there, and because it's federal parkland, no one's allowed to. A jury couldn't be formed and, as a result, you couldn't be tried.

There's a simple fix, of course—Congress could pass a law that would place Idaho's portion of the park inside the District of Idaho. But despite Kalt's efforts to get Congress to do exactly that, the loophole remains.

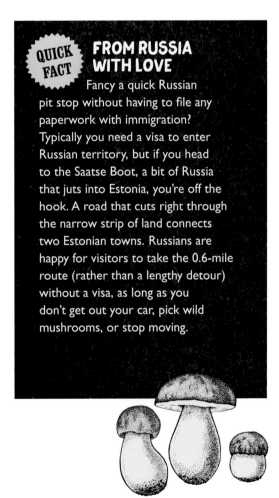

QUICK FACT

FROM RUSSIA WITH LOVE

Fancy a quick Russian pit stop without having to file any paperwork with immigration? Typically you need a visa to enter Russian territory, but if you head to the Saatse Boot, a bit of Russia that juts into Estonia, you're off the hook. A road that cuts right through the narrow strip of land connects two Estonian towns. Russians are happy for visitors to take the 0.6-mile route (rather than a lengthy detour) without a visa, as long as you don't get out your car, pick wild mushrooms, or stop moving.

88 WHICH SEA HAS NO COASTLINE?

The Sargasso Sea is situated in the North Atlantic Ocean, which makes it the only sea with no land boundary. It's measured at approximately 1,000 miles long by 3,000 miles wide—roughly two-thirds of the ocean that contains it.

COASTING ALONG

Typically, seas are found on the fringes of the oceans, and are partially enclosed by land, but the Sargasso Sea is one of a kind. Rather than being defined by land boundaries, its perimeter is determined by ocean currents. Its northern, eastern, southern, and western extremities are decided by the North Atlantic Current, the Canary Current, the North Atlantic Equatorial Current, and the Gulf Stream, respectively. While these strong currents contain the sea, the currents within it are fairly stationary, and the temperatures significantly warmer than the surrounding ocean.

SPECIAL SEAWEED

The sea is named for the large mats of dense sargassum seaweed that live on its surface. This free-floating algae is different from other types of seaweed in that it reproduces on the surface, rather than the ocean floor. It provides a diverse home for a wide variety of species, as well as a feeding ground for migratory animals that pass through it, including humpback whales and bluefin tuna. It's thought that Christopher Columbus mistook the floating patches of sargassum as an indication that he was close to land, when he was still many hundreds of miles from the shores of the Americas.

QUIZ
GEOGRAPHY

Find out how worldly wise you really are with this quick around-the-world quiz.

QUESTIONS:

1. Where is the largest segment of unclaimed land on Earth—the Arctic or Antarctica?

2. The perimeter of the Sargasso Sea is defined by ocean currents—true or false?

3. In which country is the world's highest city—Peru, Poland, or Portugal?

4. Which film director, known for blockbusters like *Titanic* and *Avatar*, has been to the bottom of the Mariana Trench?

5. The world's largest freshwater island, Marajó, is situated in the mouth of which river: the Nile, the Thames, or the Amazon?

6. Mount Everest is the tallest mountain on Earth, and Mount Chimborazo is the highest if you measure from the center of the Earth out. Which one takes longer to climb?

7. Which three states does Yellowstone National Park lie in?

8. In which country can the world's largest lake on an island be found?

9. Disappearing planes, ships, and crew members are all associated with which tropical region?

10. The Amazon River used to flow in the other direction—true or false?

Turn to page 247 for the answers.

SPORTS

89 ARE WE GETTING FASTER?

In 1935, Jesse Owens's fastest 100-meter time was 10.3 seconds. In 2009, Usain Bolt ran that distance in 9.58 seconds. It would be natural to assume our species is getting progressively faster. But the increasing speeds have more to do with technology and a wider gene pool being involved in high-profile sports.

TECH ON THE TRACK

When Jesse Owens stepped into the arena in the 1930s, he had a trowel to dig holes in the track—handmade starting blocks. The starting blocks aren't the only thing that's different today. Sports science and nutritional research have helped contemporary athletes to maximize their training regime, from high-carbohydrate gels and isotonic drinks that provide the right balance of fluid and fuel for long-distance runners, to ultra-lightweight running shoes with carbon soles and oxygen tents for a good night's sleep before a big race.

When it comes to sprinting, track technology has changed dramatically—Owens ran on cinders (pieces of rocks and burned wood), rather than the specially fabricated surface used today for running tracks. Where older tracks combine traction and shock absorption in a top layer of rubber, the latest technology separates these functions into two rubber layers: a cushioned backing to absorb the shock and a solid top layer to reduce slip and optimize traction and durability. This provides a more flexible surface, reducing the amount of time the athletes' feet are in contact with the ground. Even the spikes on runners' shoes, which were once made from steel and then ceramic, are today made from newly developed lightweight carbon nanotubes—these minimize the amount of energy absorbed by the track on impact. Analysis of Owens's joints has shown that, were he to have had the same advantages as Bolt, he would have finished only one stride behind the Jamaican legend.

THE GENE POOL

Something that is changing, however, is the gene pool of athletes competing in international competitions. As sports and sports science are introduced to new populations, and as sports have become monetized, the human bodies with the optimum physiologies to excel in each sport have come to the fore. For example, in the early 1900s, long-distance runners were largely all of the same medium build, and similar to competitors in other sports. Then Kenyan runners came on the scene in the 1980s. The country, with a population of 41 million, dominates the long-distance racing scene, along with Ethiopians and Tanzanians. The majority of the Kenyan champions come from an ethnic minority that makes up just 0.06 percent of the population, the Kalenjin. This group is known for having less body mass in relation to their height, longer legs and a shorter torso, and slender limbs. Some studies have also found a higher number of oxygen-carrying red blood cells in this group. All are characteristics advantageous for long-distance running.

90 WHAT'S THE FARTHEST SOMEONE'S TRAVELED WHILE SURFING A WAVE?

In 2016, to raise money for the Human Variome Project, Australian surfers James Cotton, Roger Gamble, and Zig Van Sluys rode the Bono tidal bore in Kampar River, Sumatra, Indonesia, for nearly 11 miles—and broke the world record for the longest surfing ride on a river bore.

EBB AND FLOW

This record was made possible by the natural tidal bore phenomenon. There are approximately 60 similar bores found around the world, caused by rising water from the world's oceans washing inland up a gradually narrowing river. On certain days of the year, when the incoming tide is highest, a vast quantity of water is forced up these estuaries, dramatically changing the volume of water in the river. The speed of the surging "top layer" of water creates a full-blown tidal wave. The Sumatran bore is known to the locals as "Seven Ghosts."

RECORD-BREAKING SURF

However, this natural wave surf pales in comparison to the 41.3 miles that Gary Saavedra from Panama spent surfing behind a wave-creating boat in 2011. That's about the same distance as from Washington, D.C. to Baltimore. He holds the Guinness World Record for the longest distance surfing a wave as well as the longest time spent surfing a wave in open water—3 hours, 55 minutes, 2 seconds. Incidentally, the farthest a dog has ever surfed is 351 feet 8 inches. The record was set by Abbie Girl, an Australian Kelpie, in San Diego, California.

91 WHAT LONG-RUNNING SPORT WAS INSPIRED BY A DOG?

When German-American acrobatic performer Nicholas Kaufmann was training on his bicycle, his beloved pet pooch got in the way. The rest is cycle-ball history . . .

FETCH THE BALL!

It was 1888 when the little-known sport of cycle-ball came to be. Kauffman's dog, Mops, ran directly into his front wheel while he was performing a balancing trick. Using the wheel, he gently maneuvered his dog out of the way. It suddenly dawned on him to replace his dog with a soccer ball and invent a whole new sport. It took a few years to get cycle-ball up and running, but the first official match was in the United States five years later. It didn't last long there, but emerged in Europe and was popular in Germany, where it became known as "radball"—*rad* means "wheel" in German.

TOTALLY RAD–BALL

The first official cycle-ball world championships took place in 1930. The sport follows similar rules to soccer, with these exceptions: players must use their bikes to pass, travel, and kick the ball, and they have to stay on their bike the whole time. Goalies are allowed to touch the ball with their hands, but they too have to stay on their bike while they do so. The sport is played indoors on a wooden floor, and the players ride heavy, single-speed bikes that are designed to be perfectly balanced. Since its early introduction there, Germany has dominated the sport, which is also played in other European countries, including Austria, Denmark, and the Czech Republic, as well as Japan and China.

92 WHAT IS THE WORLD'S MOST DANGEROUS SPORT?

Participants in BASE jumping don a wingsuit and jump at low altitudes before opening a parachute. In 2016 at least 31 people died while performing jumps, making it the deadliest year on record. In the years since, the death rate has gone down, possibly due to education and safer equipment, but it's still estimated that one out of every 2,317 jumps will end with a fatality—more than any other sport by a long shot.

NOT SO SAFE

Most people will never go BASE jumping, but the more popular triathlon's combination of swimming, cycling, and running makes it extremely dangerous. One out of every 68,515 competitors is expected to die from competing. This was based on analysis of nearly 960,000 participants, where 14 had died as a result (13 from the swimming stage of the event).

Another study at California State University, Sacramento, compared skiing and snowboarding and found that 49 percent of injured snowboarders were beginners compared to 18 percent of skiers, making it one of the most dangerous sports for novices. The risk of sustaining a head injury from skiing, however, is just as likely as with cycling and football.

NOTHING TO CHEER ABOUT

Statistics published in the *U.S. Journal of Pediatrics* in 2013 found that, in women, 66 percent of sports-caused permanent disabilities occur as a result of competitive cheerleading. Out of 26,786 high school and college cheerleading injuries in one year, 110 resulted in permanent brain injury, paralysis, or death. Disproportionately, it is the bases—the people at the bottom who support those doing the aerial acrobatics above—who end up with the life-changing injuries.

93 WHY ARE TENNIS BALLS YELLOW AND FUZZY?

Historically, tennis balls were black or white, depending on the color of the court they were used on, but in 1972 the International Tennis Federation introduced fluorescent yellow balls to the game, as research had shown that yellow was most visible for television audiences. Wimbledon stuck with the white ball, however, until 1986.

MAKE A FUZZ

The fuzzy felt coating on a tennis ball is one of its other distinctive characteristics. While it may make the balls seem less intimidating, its true purpose is all to do with aerodynamics. The ball's surface affects its speed as it flies through the air—the fuzzier the ball, the slower its speed. That's why professional tennis players often inspect multiple balls before deciding on one to serve with—they're looking for a ball where a lot of the fuzz is lying flat against the ball's surface, for maximum speed and spin.

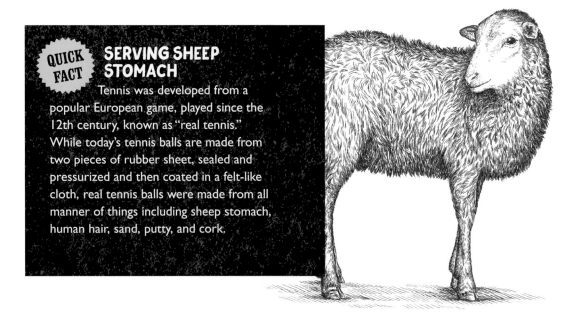

QUICK FACT

SERVING SHEEP STOMACH

Tennis was developed from a popular European game, played since the 12th century, known as "real tennis." While today's tennis balls are made from two pieces of rubber sheet, sealed and pressurized and then coated in a felt-like cloth, real tennis balls were made from all manner of things including sheep stomach, human hair, sand, putty, and cork.

94 WHAT DO A WAFFLE IRON AND SNEAKERS HAVE IN COMMON?

Blue Ribbon Sports was founded in 1964. Its owners were Bill Bowerman, a track and field coach at the University of Oregon, and alumnus Phil Knight, and they distributed sneakers for a Japanese manufacturer. In 1971, Bowerman had an idea for an innovative shoe—and Blue Ribbon Sports became Nike Inc.

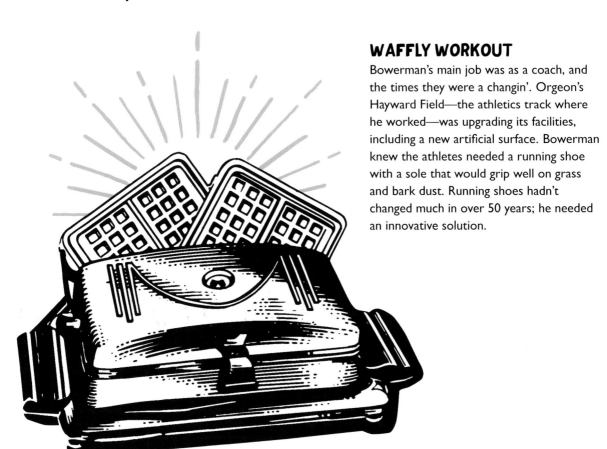

WAFFLY WORKOUT

Bowerman's main job was as a coach, and the times they were a changin'. Orgeon's Hayward Field—the athletics track where he worked—was upgrading its facilities, including a new artificial surface. Bowerman knew the athletes needed a running shoe with a sole that would grip well on grass and bark dust. Running shoes hadn't changed much in over 50 years; he needed an innovative solution.

THE NIKE "SWOOSH"

In 1971, the year Blue Ribbon became Nike, a young graphic design student named Carolyn Davidson was paid $35 by Phil Knight to come up with a logo for the new shoe brand. She was working for him on a $2-an-hour rate and spent just 17.5 hours coming up with the design. Davidson's Nike "swoosh" has become one of the most recognized logos in the world. She later received a significant number of shares from Nike, worth hundreds of thousands of dollars. Not bad for a few days' work.

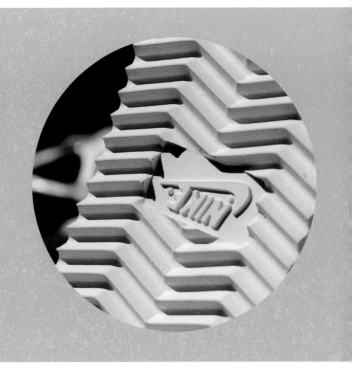

The conundrum was on his mind one morning over breakfast when his wife was making waffles. The waffle iron's pattern proved to be that inspiration.

Bowerman had a home laboratory, and according to his wife Barbara, "He got up from the table and went tearing into his lab and got two cans of whatever it is you pour together to make the urethane, and poured them into the waffle iron." The rubber mold created from the waffle iron would be used as the inspiration for Nike's first shoe: the Waffle Trainer. The raised nubs created by the waffle-inspired mold would become Bowerman's first patent—he ended up with a total of eight. His designs would go on to inspire other classic Nike shoes, including the Nike Cortez and the Moon Shoe.

UNEARTHED TREASURES

So what became of the waffle iron used to make those first prototype soles? It was thrown into the trash heap in the Bowermans' backyard. The garbage truck would not come to their house, so the family would bury their trash in a pit out in the back, and the destroyed waffle iron went in that pit too. But in 2011, when one of Bowerman's sons was looking to remodel the family's shop, he excavated the yard to pour a new foundation. That was when the 6-inch, 1930s waffle iron, which had been a wedding gift to the Bowermans, emerged from the soil. The family contacted Nike and traded the iron for sporting equipment for a local athletics program.

95 WHO WAS RESPONSIBLE FOR THE FIRST BASKETBALL "SWISH"?

A "swish" in basketball is when a player makes a shot through the hoop where the ball doesn't touch the rim or the backboard—it simply passes right through the net, making that swishing sound that players and fans love to hear. But there was a time when basketballs didn't swish.

THE SOUND OF SUCCESS

Basketball was invented in 1891 by Dr. James Naismith. But there was an obvious reason it was called "basket" ball. The original game was played with two peach baskets fixed to posts or the balconies of running tracks in indoor sports facilities. Nets began to make an appearance in 1893, but even then they were still metal and closed-ended, so players had to fish out the ball each time to continue play—no swishes there. Over 20 years after the game was first played, in 1912, open-ended fabric nets became approved for use in high school and college games.

THE SWISH IN WRITING

The first real-life recorded swish (swishes were written about in fiction as early as 1913) is believed to belong to a Brooklyn player named George Edelstein. A writer in the *New York Tribune* observed the Bushwick High School player had only four shots where he failed to "send the ball swishing through the basket for a point." And so the swish was born.

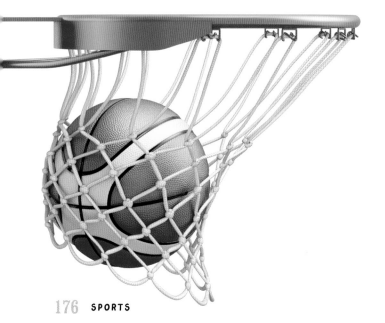

WHERE WAS TABLE TENNIS INVENTED?

Table tennis is an international sport of agility, speed, and skill, but its origins lie in the after-dinner amusements of British soldiers stationed abroad in the late 1800s. Then it wasn't known as table tennis, or even Ping-Pong, but by the whimsical name "whiff-whaff."

AFTER-DINNER DALLIANCE

There's a dispute about the precise birthplace of table tennis—the military mess halls of India, Malaysia, or Asia Minor are all candidates. In an attempt to bring the popularity of tennis to an indoor setting, soldiers and the English gentry would hit a wine cork back and forth across a table using cigar box lids. The net was a wall of stacked books. Thus, the game could be played anywhere, with anything, and by anyone. Around the world, many languages refer to the sport literally as table tennis. In French it's *tennis de table*, in German *tischtennis*, in Dutch *tafeltennis*, and in Norweigan *bordtennis*. But in Chinese, the phonetic pronunciation *Pingpang qiú* is more similar to "Ping-Pong."

PING-PONG TAKES OFF

In 1901, the Jacques games company trademarked the name "Ping-Pong" after the sound the new celluloid ball made when it hit the table and the rackets (also known as paddles and bats), which had a solid wooden frame and handle and were covered with stretched vellum. Soon, standardized rules were introduced and the two rival associations—the Table Tennis Association and the Ping-Pong Association—united in 1903 to form one governing body. Later introductions of sponge-coated rackets with rubber top layers transformed table tennis into the fast-paced sport we know today.

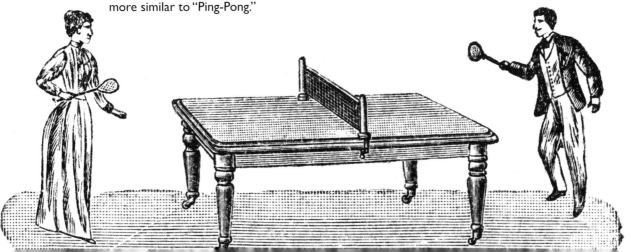

97 CAN YOU WIN AN OLYMPIC MEDAL FOR PAINTING?

You're unlikely to see an Olympic competitor wielding a paintbrush anytime soon, but for the first 40 years of the modern Olympics, it wasn't all that uncommon.

ON YOUR MARKS, GET SET, PAINT!

From 1912 to 1952, Olympic Games juries awarded official medals for painting, sculpture, architecture, literature, and music. Over the period, some 151 medals were handed out to artistic talents—re-creating the categories of achievements originally celebrated by the ancient Greeks.

INSPIRING PERSPIRING

At first, local organizers weren't keen to incorporate the arts alongside athletics, but by the time the 1912 Stockholm Games came around, there was enough support for the events as long as the entered artworks were inspired by sport. The first gold-medal winners included a piece of music entitled "Olympic Triumphal March" and a painting depicting winter sports. However, professional artists were prohibited from entering, which meant there were few well-known winners, and sometimes the juries could find no entrants worthy of a medal. Notable winners included Italian sculptor Rembrandt Bugatti and Dutch painter Isaac Israëls.

WINS FOR THE HOME TEAM

One of the most successful Olympic art competitions was undoubtedly the 1936 Games in Berlin. More than 70,000 arts enthusiasts visited the event's accompanying exhibition, and artworks were purchased by celebrity citizens and visitors, including Third Reich minister Joseph Goebbels. As the Minister of Propaganda, Goebbels used the competition to boost Nazi policy and ideals of racial supremacy.

In the months leading up to the Olympics, some countries were still threatening to skip the Games altogether because of Nazi policies—German Jewish athletes had been banned from taking part—although 49 teams ultimately ended up going to Berlin. The art event's "international" jury consisted of 29 German judges and just 12 from other European countries. The jury's favor for German artists meant the country received a much-needed increase in their overall medal haul, winning five of the nine available.

FIVE QUICK FACTS

 1

THEY ONCE SHOT REAL PIGEONS IN THE OLYMPICS

The 1900 Summer Games in Paris was notable for the fact that it was the only Games to feature live pigeon shooting, with hundreds of birds being slaughtered in the name of sport.

 2

THE WORLD'S LARGEST BOWLING ALLEY IS IN JAPAN

Opened in 1972 and measuring 650 feet in length, Inazawa Grand Bowl in Inazawa, Japan, has a record-breaking 116 lanes.

 3

ONE OLYMPIC QUALIFYING SOCCER MATCH TURNED DEADLY

The 1964 qualifying game between Peru and Argentina included a particularly controversial referee decision. The crowd stormed the field, but because the stadium gates were locked when a stampede ensued, 328 people were killed.

 4

THE STANLEY CUP IS BAD AT SPELLING

It's ice hockey's highest accolade, but the trophy is renowned for its many spelling mistakes, including a number of winning players' names and BOSTON being spelled BQSTQN.

 5

THIS PLAYER COULDN'T PLAY IN SPACE

When British soccer team Sunderland signed Swede Stefan Schwarz in 1999, his contract stipulated that he couldn't travel to space on a commercial passenger flight.

98 WHY IS THE TOUR DE FRANCE'S YELLOW JERSEY YELLOW?

You don't need to be a big fan of the Tour de France to know that the cyclist leading the overall race wears the yellow jersey—the garment has become synonymous with the sport. But it wasn't always so. Despite the race being around since 1903, the jersey didn't make its first appearance until 1919.

MAKING HIS MARK

The first person to wear the yellow jersey, or *maillot jaune*, was French rider Eugène Christophe. The year was 1919, and it was the first time the Tour had taken place since 1914. World War I had brought destruction and devastation to the people of France, and it was decided that the Tour, which had quickly become a hugely popular event, was what was needed to boost the morale of the people. While today's riders covet the yellow jersey, in 1919 Eugène Christophe was less keen, claiming it made him an easier mark for the other riders. Unfortunately, despite wearing the jersey for 10 of the Tour's 15 stages (there are now 21 one-day segments completed over 23 days), Christophe lost the winning spot to Belgian Firmin Lambot, finishing third on the podium.

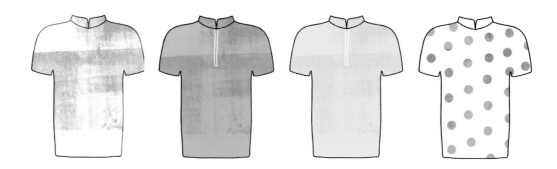

COLORS OF THE TOUR

The yellow jersey might be the most recognizable, but it's not the only special jersey that features in the Tour. Continuing in order of jersey ranking, there's the green jersey, awarded to the rider leading the points classification; the polka-dot jersey, worn by the "King of the Mountains" for the rider with the best climber ranking; and the white jersey, worn by the highest general classification-ranked rider under the age of 26. If a rider is leading in more than one classification, he wears whichever jersey is ranked higher.

WHY YELLOW?

The Tour was put on by *L'Auto*, a sports magazine that began the stage race as a way to boost circulation. Prior to 1919, the race leader would wear a yellow armband to signify his position. But this made it hard for fans to pick him out from the side of the road, so it was suggested to the magazine's editor, Henri Desgrange, that a colored jersey might make more sense. It's believed that yellow was chosen to reflect the color of the paper that *L'Auto* was printed on, but legend also has it that Desgrange needed 15 jerseys—one for each stage of the race—and that the supplier only had that number available in yellow, the least popular color.

JERSEY RULES

The yellow jersey is worn by whichever rider is leading the general classification after the previous day's stage. In other words, they are the leader of the overall time ranking when their times from all completed stages are added together. Even if you don't win the overall race, if you've worn a yellow jersey at any point in the Tour, you get to keep it as a souvenir. But wearing the jersey doesn't guarantee victory. Fabian Cancellara has spent 29 days wearing the yellow jersey, across six Tours, without ever winning the overall race.

99 WHAT DO YOU DO IN A *DOJO*?

Kyudo, meaning "the way of the bow," is an ancient Japanese discipline dating to 250 BC. It is practiced in a special hall called a *kyudojo*, or *dojo* for short, and the process of learning and preparing to shoot a bow is meditative and spiritual—it's heavily influenced by Shinto and Zen Buddhism.

THE WAY OF THE BOW

There are eight stages to shooting a bow using the *kyudo* technique, and even the correct stance can take a long time to master. Archers must spread their feet the distance of one arrow length, called *yazuka*, with their big toes lined up with the center of the target. *Hikiwake*, meaning "drawing the bow," sees the archer draw the bow at forehead height, before lowering it to mouth level to release. *Dojo* members take it in turns to shoot at the target—the least experienced go first, followed by the highly skilled archers.

ARCHERY AT THE OLYMPICS

Target archery has been included in every Olympic Games since 1972. Archers have just 40 seconds to shoot six arrows at a target positioned 230 feet away. The target's central circle, the bull's-eye, measures just 4.8 inches across. When the bow is released, the arrow travels at speeds of 150 miles per hour. Olympic archers use a recurve bow, where both ends of the bow curve away from the archer when it's unstrung.

QUIZ

SPORTS

You've put the training in; now it's time to stretch your muscles and claim the title by taking this quiz!

QUESTIONS:

1. Basketball was originally played using two peach baskets instead of hoops and nets—true or false?

2. What breakfast food inspired the soles of Nike's first shoe?

3. In archery, what is the target's central circle called?

4. Natural waves created by rising oceans washing inland up a gradually narrowing river are known as: tidal yawns, tidal bores, or tidal stretches?

5. In which year were the Olympic Games held in Berlin?

6. What is BASE jumping?

7. Yellow tennis balls were introduced after research showed players could hit them faster—true or false?

8. What was the name of the dog whose owner invented cycle-ball?

9. What did Jesse Owens need a trowel for when he walked out onto the running tracks in the 1930s?

10. The rider leading the general classification in the Tour de France wears a polka-dot jersey—true or false?

Turn to page 248 for the answers.

SCIENCE

100 WHAT'S THE WORLD'S MOST DANGEROUS CHEMICAL?

New chemicals are being created and discovered on a regular basis. Often, scientists can guess at the reactions that will occur, based on a chemical's properties. Other times, as was the case with the following contenders for the world's scariest chemical, they get a nasty surprise.

SUBSTANCE N–0 WAY

If the Nazis considered something too dangerous, you know to be very, very afraid. Chlorine trifluoride (ClF_3) was discovered in the 1930s in Germany, and a few years later it became a subject of study at the Kaiser Wilhelm Institute, where the Third Reich conducted a number of scientific experiments. Dubbed *N-stoff* or "substance N" by those researching it, there was no denying the chemical's remarkable properties. It produces a toxic gas at boiling point, which is a mere 53.15°F; it ignites easily and burns at over 7,866°F; it's highly corrosive; and it explodes on contact with water. The Nazis planned to produce 55 tons of substance N every month, and use it to destroy their enemies. One plan involved putting it in flamethrowers to dowse whole cities in the lethal weapon. However, the chemical's volatile nature was also its downfall—it would even eat through the flamethrower before the weapon could be used—so the Nazis only produced about 55 tons of the stuff in total. Even the brains at NASA couldn't figure out how to harness its properties. Packing so much power, they thought it might make the perfect propellant for launching rockets, but after a 1950s spillage ate through a steel tank, a concrete floor, and about 3 feet of gravel underneath, they changed their minds.

WHAT'S THAT SMELL?

An extremely stinky chemical might not sound scary, but thioacetone (C_3H_6S) was responsible for the evacuation of an entire city. In 1889, scientists in Freiberg, Germany, who were working with the chemical reported "an offensive smell which spread rapidly over a great area of the town, causing fainting, vomiting, and a panic evacuation." The chemical is so potent that one drop can be smelled from a third of a mile away. In the 1960s, two chemists made the mistake of leaving a stopper off a bottle of the stuff while experimenting with it as part of an investigation into new polymers at the Esso Research Station in Abingdon, UK. They couldn't escape the stench and received a deodorant dosing from a waitress when they went out for dinner.

SUPER ACID

Insane explosives and unbearable odors aside, there's nothing more terrifying than a highly corrosive acid. Perhaps the world's strongest is fluoroantimonic acid (H_2FSbF_6). It's so strong it can eat through glass, plastic, and any living organism, including bone. That might sound scary, but in order to store it safely you just need a container made from polytetrafluoroethylene, otherwise known as Teflon.

101 CAN YOU SMELL YOUR DINNER WITH YOUR TONGUE?

Until recently, traditional thinking asserted that we use our noses to sense smell and our tongues to taste, but a recent study has turned some of that thinking on its head, literally.

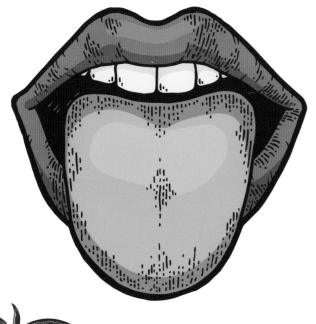

ON THE NOSE

The notion of five distinct senses is something we're all taught in school, and it was widely thought that taste and smell were independent systems by the scientific community too. But when cell biologist Mehmet Hakan Ozdener's 12-year-old son asked him if snakes extend their tongues so they can smell, it sparked an idea. Together with scientists at the Monell Chemical Senses Center in Philadelphia, he tested genetically modified mice to pinpoint the location of olfactory receptors—the ones we use to experience smell. In the mice, they found that these receptors were present in taste cells.

TASTE SENSATION

Then, testing living human taste cells in culture, using genetic and biochemical methods, they found similar results—the cells contained many important molecules that are found in olfactory receptors. The team was surprised to discover that these human taste cells responded to fragrances, even when the concentration of a scent was below the level required to trigger a taste

response. While it's not yet known whether the information from these receptors gets sent straight to the brain, or whether it's combined in your mouth, it's a strong indication that your tongue is partly responsible for how things smell to you. But this isn't the first time olfactory receptors have been found somewhere other than the nose—they're located in many tissues, including sperm cells, where they seem to help guide the reproductive cells to the egg.

SCENT OF THE WILD

And what about that intrigued 12-year-old's question? Although snakes do have nostrils, they rely much more heavily on their tongues for sensory information, including spatial awareness. They flick that little forked muscle around outside, capturing scent molecules, before drawing it back into the roof of the mouth. That's where the molecules are transferred to the snake's sensory center, helping them make sense of the world.

FAVORITE FLAVOR

When you enjoy a bit of your favorite sandwich or a lick of delicious ice cream, taste is how your brain detects whether sweet, salty, sour, bitter, or umami (savory) molecules are present on your tongue. But it's your sense of smell that gives you the detailed information about the quality of the food's flavor—that's how you know you're eating vanilla or white chocolate, raspberry or strawberry, for example. This scientific development isn't suggesting that if you open up your mouth and hold it up to an apple pie you'll be able to take a whiff, but it might open doors to the possibility of injecting low levels of odor into a food to trick our brain into thinking it's sweeter than it is, reducing the need for real sugar—a potential strategy for dealing with obesity.

WHY IS YAWNING CONTAGIOUS?

Seeing a picture of a yawn or even talking about yawning is enough to provoke a gaping-mouth stretch of significant proportions in some people—and it seems that the more empathetic you are, the more likely you are to launch into a yawn whenever you see others doing so.

IT'S CATCHING

There are a number of theories as to why humans yawn when they see others doing it, but mimicry is one that holds a lot of weight. As social creatures, empathy— the ability to feel and understand the emotions of others—plays an important part in our social cohesion. When we see others smiling or laughing, we tend to smile or laugh, and the same is true for frowning

or sad expressions. Research at the Yerkes National Primate Research Center at Emory University indicates that contagious yawning may just be a by-product of an empathetic nature.

About 60–70 percent of people are susceptible to contagious yawning, and the research shows it occurs most often in individuals who score highly on empathetic tests. Scans of the brain show that the areas activated during contagious yawning are the same areas involved in the processing of our own emotions and those of other people. And we're not the only species to do it. This catching behavior has been observed in chimpanzees and bonobos.

THE YAWNING MYTH

Being tired or bored, and the sight of someone else doing it, can all trigger a yawn, but what does the body get in return for this often socially awkward response? The reason often cited is that it's our body's way of increasing oxygen to the bloodstream. But science has turned up no evidence as yet that yawning increases the levels of oxygen in the blood. Other theories suggest that it's a primitive form of communication used to alert the group to tiredness, setting everyone's bodies to the same sleep pattern; or that the strenuous stretch of the face is making you more alert when you're sleepy or more focused when you're distracted.

COOL OFF

However, the one prevailing school of thought is that yawning helps to regulate brain temperature. A 2007 study at SUNY College, Oneonta, found that when a hot pack was held to a participant's forehead, they yawned 41 percent of the time, compared to 9 percent for cold packs. The brain heats up more than other organs, and the gaping mouth of a yawn means a bigger gulp of air is inhaled, which travels to our upper nasal and oral cavities. The blood vessels in these areas head straight up to the brain, cooling it off. The jaw stretch also increases the rate of blood flow, so the brain can benefit from that rush of cool air more efficiently. Before we fall asleep and when we wake up are the times of day that our brain and body temperatures are at their highest, which would explain why we tend to yawn most at these times.

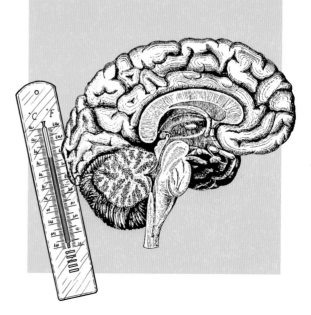

103 WHY IS CHOCOLATE BAD FOR DOGS?

Cocoa contains a molecule called theobromine, which is very toxic to dogs. Chemically speaking, it's similar to caffeine. Consumed in small doses, this molecule can increase your heart rate and the amount of oxygen and nutrients to your brain. But how does it affect dogs?

CANDY CATASTROPHE

Despite being man's best friend, dogs are very different from us—their bodies don't metabolize theobromine very well. This means the effects that are minimal to us last a lot longer in a dog's central nervous system. When dogs eat chocolate, they can develop theobromine poisoning. The symptoms, which include a high temperature, seizures, vomiting, heavy panting, and diarrhea, can take up to 12 hours to set in.

Dark chocolate (with cocoa percentages of 70 percent and above), baking chocolate, and cocoa powder have higher concentrations of theobromine, so are more harmful to dogs. For a dog weighing 44 pounds to consume a deadly dose of theobromine, it would have to devour well over 6 pounds of milk chocolate. Considering your average candy bar weighs about $1^3/4$ ounces, Fido would have to chow down on about 60 bars for it to have a lethal effect.

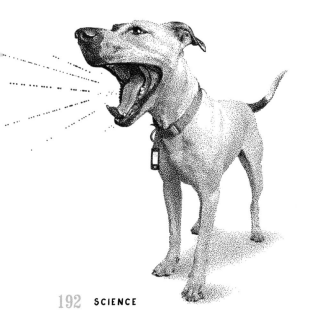

FREAKISH FELINES

Despite its toxic nature, most dogs love the taste of chocolate and can't get enough, with small dogs more likely to feel the effects. Their purring pals, however, are unlikely to seek out the deadly delicacy. Why? That's because the taste receptors in cats' tongues aren't configured like ours or dogs'—they can't taste anything sweet, because they lack one of the genes required to do so.

104 WHY DOES CUTTING AN ONION MAKE YOU CRY?

When tears are streaming from your eyes next time you're making dinner, it might seem like the onions are exacting their revenge for sacrificing them for your meal, but in fact that gas is created by the sulfur that onions absorb from the soil.

SOBBING SULFUR

Slicing into an onion splits open its cells, causing a chemical reaction that releases a gas called syn-Propanethial-S-oxide—a combination of special enzymes and sulfenic acid. When the sensory nerves in the front of your eyes detect this invasive compound, a message is sent to your central nervous system, which you experience as a burning sensation. A signal is then sent to your tear-producing glands to wash out the irritant gas, and you get all weepy—but when you banish the pesky onions to a hot pan, the heat deactivates the enzymes.

THE "NO-TEARS" ONION

One British farmer made headlines in 2015 when he announced the development of a red onion variety that does not trigger tears. Twenty years in the making, the farmer claimed the "Sweet Red" variety had lower pungency levels than regular onions, making it easier on your eyes—and on your breath!

It's thought that this lachrymator gas is produced to deter the plant's herbivore predators. Onion tears can be avoided by chilling the vegetable in the refrigerator first—the cold impacts some of the onion's gas-inducing compounds. There is an upside to the tears, though: those sulfur compounds give onions their unique flavor.

105 IS THE PERIODIC TABLE COMPLETE?

In late 2015, scientists rejoiced at the completion of the seventh row of the periodic table of elements after the results of years of experiments were confirmed by the International Union of Pure and Applied Chemistry (IUPAC). This opened up the invitation to begin the next row—but will scientists eventually stop discovering new elements?

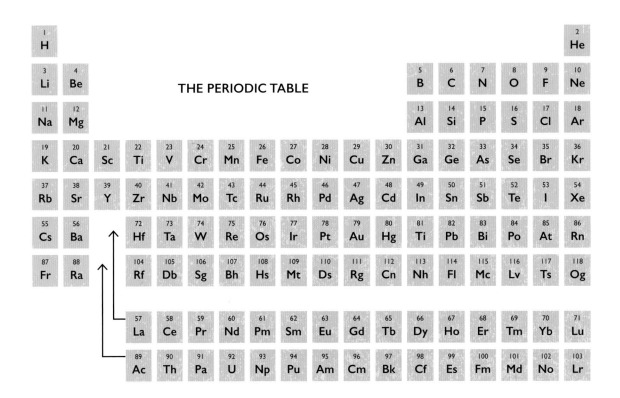

THE PERIODIC TABLE

A SEAT AT THE TABLE

The periodic table organizes elements by rows and columns. The rows, called periods, are based on their atomic number—in other words, the number of protons in an atom's nucleus—and the columns, called groups, are based on the orbits of their outermost electrons. These orbits inform the personality of the element, so elements in the same group tend to behave similarly. For example, all the elements in group one are alkali metals that are soft and highly reactive, such as lithium, sodium, and rubidium.

Na
sodium

Uranium, with an atomic number of 92, is the last element on the table that's stable enough to occur naturally on Earth. Every other element beyond it is only studied by smashing together lighter atoms to create heavier ones, and then searching through the decay to identify heavier elements. Scientists have calculated that they may be able to discover elements up to an atomic number of 173, but this process currently has its limitations. It's possible that much heavier elements exist inside stars and elsewhere in the universe, making the table far from complete.

NEW DISCOVERIES

It's IUPAC's job to make the final decision about the names and symbols for each new element, and in the last few years they've been busy adding four new elements to the table. The discovery of 113, 115, 117, and 118 by scientists in Russia, Japan, and the United States was confirmed at the end of 2015, completing the seventh row of the table. They have since been officially named nihonium (Nh), moscovium (Mc), tennessine (Ts), and oganesson (Og), respectively. The discovery of these synthetic elements took years and was only possible in a laboratory, where they existed for a fraction of a second. Work is already underway to discover 119 and 120.

SWEDISH SYMBOLS

Prior to the systematic classification in place today, various symbols were used for different elements, but as the number of known elements grew, a more ordered method became essential. Swedish chemist Jöns Jacob Berzelius assigned many of the symbol letters in the early 19th century, and his method became accepted around the world. Most elements' symbols are made from the first letter or first two letters of their name, such as oxygen (O), nitrogen (N), aluminum (Al), and nickel (Ni). But where elements have the same first two initials, they deviate from this pattern: for example, calcium (Ca) and cadmium (Cd). Some symbols are derived from the element's Latin name. Gold, for example, has the symbol Au from the Latin *aurum*, and copper is Cu from *cuprum*.

106 WHAT MAKES BACON SMELL SO DELICIOUS?

Bacon is the one thing many vegetarians would shun their meat-free lives for. And it's no surprise—the distinct aroma of frying bacon draws people to the kitchen like moths to a flame. Scientists have found that over 150 chemicals combine to create the unique smell that gets your mouth watering.

BROWNING BRILLIANCE

When bacon is sizzling in the pan, there's a whole lot of chemistry going on. First, there's the Maillard reaction—it's what makes things turn brown when you cook them. It's caused when the bacon is heated and the amino acids it contains react with the natural sugars, breaking them down. Other compounds are given off from the breaking down of bacon fat.

THE ULTIMATE CURE

One thing that sets the smell of fried bacon apart from other cooked pork products is the fact that it's been cured. While aroma compounds such as pyridine, pyrazine, and furans are found in both fried bacon and fried pork loin, these meaty-smelling molecules are dramatically increased with the presence of nitrites, which are used in the curing process of bacon. When the nitrites in bacon fat are heated, they create more nitrogen-containing compounds found exclusively in bacon, including 2,5-dimethylpyrazine, 2,3-dimethylpyrazine, 2-ethyl-5-methylpyrazine, and 2-ethyl-3,5-dimethylpyrazine. Scientists believe it's the combination of these that give bacon its unique aroma.

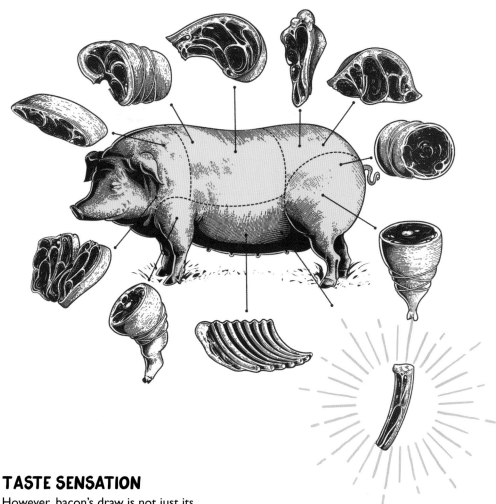

TASTE SENSATION

However, bacon's draw is not just its smell. The taste is what keeps people coming back for more. The flavor, like the aroma, is created by a combination of elements. One of the major factors is the result of the pork belly's fat breaking down. Classes of molecules, such as aldehydes, furans, and ketones, are created by the breakdown of fatty acids in the muscle tissue and combine to create the unique flavor. If any were missing, bacon would not taste as it does. But not all bacon is alike, and the breed of pig the bacon is derived from, and what that pig was fed on, affect the type of fatty acids that are present, and therefore the molecules that result when they're broken down.

A MOUTHFUL OF MOUTHFEEL

Finally, bacon's draw is something known as "mouthfeel"—the way certain foods feel in the mouth. Crispy bacon provides a stark contrast to the foods it's usually served with—pancakes, eggs, and potatoes. This texture combination satisfies the brain's craving for novelty, increasing the amount of pleasure you experience when you eat it. The melt-in-the-mouth nature of bacon also makes it very moreish. Known as "vanishing caloric density," your brain is tricked into thinking you're eating fewer calories than you are, urging you to eat more.

WHY ARE THERE SO MANY TWINS IN INDIA'S "TWIN TOWN"?

In the southern Indian state of Kerala lies a small town with an unusually high number of twins, but despite luring researchers keen to uncover the population's secret, the cause remains a mystery.

SEEING DOUBLE

Kodinhi has a population of 11,000, but 1,000 twins and counting. That makes it the place with the highest number of twins per capita anywhere in the world. Twins account for 42 of every 1,000 births, which is about six times as high as the global average. Unlike Western countries, where multiple embryos can be transplanted in IVF treatment, leading to a much higher chance of twin births, women in Kodinhi are conceiving naturally, aren't using contraceptive pills, and don't use oral medications to promote ovulation.

IN TWO MINDS

The rise in the twin population started over half a century ago, but it's only recently that scientists have been trying to figure out the cause. The twins are born to both Muslim and Hindu families, and reportedly to women who have moved from other communities. A joint team of researchers from India, Germany, and the UK have collected saliva samples from the town's twins in an effort to find a genetic reason for the sudden twin frenzy. Other studies have focused instead on height and weight, facial profiles, and the twins' teeth to try to find an answer. In other small communities with high twin populations, such as Igbo ora in Nigeria and Cândido Godói in Brazil, the diet and inbreeding respectively were believed to be the cause, but in Kodinhi, results are still inconclusive.

108 WHAT CAUSED HALLUCINATIONS IN PONT-SAINT-ESPRIT?

In the summer of 1961, something strange started happening to the residents of the southern French town of Pont-Saint-Esprit—was bad bread the cause, or was it something more sinister?

TRAIL OF BREAD CRUMBS

That August, more than 250 people experienced bizarre symptoms—overwhelming nausea and wild hallucinations gripped the sleepy riverside town. Five people died and many more became gravely ill—one man, thinking he was a plane, jumped out of his window on the second floor, breaking both his legs. The town's doctors at the time concluded that one of the bakeries had become contaminated with ergot, a poisonous fungus that can occur naturally on rye, but nearly 50 years later a book hoped to shed new light on what, or rather who, might have really been responsible.

INTELLIGENCE BAKED IN

In 2009, journalist Hank P. Albarelli Jr. discovered a CIA document labeled "Re: Pont-Saint-Esprit and F. Olson Files [. . .] Hand carry to Belin—tell him to see to it that these are buried." F. Olson most likely stands for Frank Olson, a CIA scientist who led research into the mind-altering drug LSD. And Belin was David Belin—executive director of a commission set up to investigate CIA abuses. Albarelli theorizes that these "buried" files would reveal that the CIA was experimenting with LSD on the town's hapless residents, perhaps by sneaking it into the local bakery's bread. It's now known that the CIA, fearful that communist regimes were using LSD to brainwash captured Americans, carried out experiments on their own citizens, so it's not a big stretch to think that this quiet French town fell foul of the same unscrupulous behavior.

109 IS THE DEAD SEA DEAD?

When divers went looking for the cause of mysterious surface ripples, they discovered that some things in the Dead Sea's murky depths are alive and kicking.

A PINCH OF SALT

The Dead Sea is a tough spot for most living things to set up home. About 3.5 percent of ocean waters are made up of dissolved minerals, known as "salts." But because the Dead Sea (technically a lake) is landlocked and located in the lowest valley on Earth, it acts as a repository for minerals from the freshwater rivers and streams that collect in it. With no outlet, the water can only escape by evaporating, leaving the salty minerals behind. Over time, this caused the lake to be nearly nine times saltier than ocean water.

DEEP-DIVE DISCOVERY

In 2010, a diving expedition to explore dozens of craters at the bottom of the lake, some measuring 33 feet wide and 43 feet deep, revealed that there was life there after all. The craters, created by springs which spew fresh water, were covered with green and white biofilms of new, diverse bacterial species.

BOBBING ALONG

All that salt means the Dead Sea has become a popular tourist destination, with visitors swimming—or rather floating—in the waters for pleasure and to help cure health problems. Objects stop sinking when they displace a mass of water equal to their body mass, but salty water is more dense, so only a small amount of it needs to be displaced to match your body mass. When you get in, a lot of your body stays out of the water, and it can be hard to dive under it or put your feet down.

DEADLY WATERS

If it's so hard to submerge yourself, then why is it considered one of the most dangerous places to go swimming in Israel? For exactly that reason. If you're floating on your back, you're fine. But if you accidentally flip over, you could find yourself in a lot of trouble. In less salty water, you could push your feet down to lift your head, but that's not the case in the Dead Sea. If no one's there to help, you might struggle to get your head out of the water in time. And that's not the only issue you have to consider—highly saline water can burn your eyes and is extremely poisonous if swallowed. The salt causes the larynx to inflate, causing choking and suffocation.

FIVE QUICK FACTS

1 THE SUN IS GETTING HOTTER

In 2.3 billion years it will be too hot for any life to exist on Earth—the extreme temperatures will have evaporated the oceans, transforming Earth into a Mars-like desert.

2 SOIL IS RICH WITH LIFE

One tiny teaspoon of soil contains more microorganisms than there are people on the planet. That's millions of species and billions of bacteria, algae, microscopic insects, and more.

3 MORE THAN HALF THE OXYGEN WE BREATHE IS PRODUCED BY MARINE LIFE

While land-dwelling plants are important too, plankton, seaweed, and other marine plants are responsible for photosynthesizing the oxygen we need to breathe.

4 THE PERIODIC TABLE DOESN'T CONTAIN THE LETTER J

It's the only letter not found in the table. "Q" also doesn't appear in any official element names, but it does feature in temporary element names.

5 OUR BODIES COULD MAKE PENCILS

The human body contains a lot of carbon—about 35 pounds—which is enough to make graphite for about 9,000 pencils.

110 HOW DO FORENSIC INVESTIGATORS FIND TRACES OF BLOOD (AND HORSERADISH) AT A CRIME SCENE?

Crime-show junkies know that mopping up a pool of blood is never going to fully cover a murderer's tracks. When TV investigators arrive at the crime scene, they usually spray everything with a liquid, illuminating blood stains the criminal thought no one would ever find. So what's in the spray bottle?

ILLUMINATING THE PROBLEM

The bottle usually contains luminol—a powdery compound that's made up of nitrogen, hydrogen, oxygen, and carbon. It's mixed together with other chemicals, including hydrogen peroxide and sodium hydroxide, and sprayed where investigators think traces of blood might be hiding. A chemical reaction is caused when the luminol is sprayed on hemoglobin—the oxygen-carrying protein in blood. The chemicals break down the molecules in the hemoglobin, which emit energy in the form of light photons, creating a pale blue luminescence when the room is dark. Even if the blood has been washed away, traces of up to one part per million can be detected by luminol.

TRUE CRIME

In reality, unlike the glow you normally see on TV, that pale blue evidence will only glow for around 30 seconds, and spraying luminol can also smear blood impressions, damaging evidence. Despite its effectiveness, the method is not foolproof, as other things can be the catalyst for the same glowing reaction. Chemicals in bleach, urine with blood in it, feces, and even enzymes in horseradish can cause a false positive.

111 WHY DO LEAVES CHANGE COLOR IN THE FALL?

Every fall, almost like clockwork, leaves on trees are transformed from their usual luscious greens to a warming palette of yellows, oranges, and reds. Behind this autumnal artistry lies some clever chemistry.

GOING GREEN

Chlorophyll is the chemical compound that creates the typical green color present in most leaves. It's an important component in photosynthesis—the process by which plants convert energy from sunlight into carbon dioxide, and water into sugars. As winter approaches and the days get darker, sunshine is in short supply, and so the production of chlorophyll slows down. Existing chlorophyll in the leaves decomposes. But the change from green to yellow, orange, or red is not the chlorophyll decomposing, but rather the other compounds in the leaves, always present but usually less dominant, showing their true colors.

SEEING RED

Other pigment families found in leaves include carotenoids and flavonoids, which create yellow hues, while carotenoids also lead to oranges and reds. These decompose more slowly than chlorophyll, so it becomes possible to see them as the chlorophyll diminishes. In plants with red or purple leaves, the dominant pigment compounds are anthocyanins. These aren't typically found year-round, but their production is triggered by an increased concentration of sugar in the leaves, caused by darker days. The advantages of anthocyanins are not fully understood, but theories suggest their antioxidant properties protect the plant as it prepares for winter.

112 CAN YOU UNBOIL AN EGG?

Scientists might not have figured out how we can live on the Moon, but they have solved one of breakfast's most important mysteries. Yes, it is possible to unboil an egg—at least, the white of it.

HOW DO YOU LIKE YOUR EGGS?

Eggs are protein-rich, and these proteins, like others, are made up of amino acids—building blocks arranged in a specific way, giving the protein its unique shape and useful properties. When these proteins are subjected to an increase in temperature, the connections are disrupted, causing the protein to unravel and tangle. This is what causes an egg to go from clear to white when boiled.

At the University of California, Irvine, research chemists added a urea substance to cooked egg whites. This waste product chewed away at the whites, returning the solid egg to a liquid. They then used a special vortex fluid device, which stressed the proteins back into their original formation.

PROTEIN POWER

These scientists weren't trying to figure this out just for fun. Their research has lots of underlying implications for cutting the costs of food production and for cancer treatments, among other things. Vast amounts of money are spent on reversing the misfolding process caused when proteins are formed, or preventing it in the first place. For example, to make cancer antibodies, scientists use hamster ovary cells, which don't misfold proteins. This new method is fast, reduces waste, and has the potential to save industries the $160 billion spent on proteins each year.

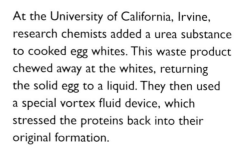

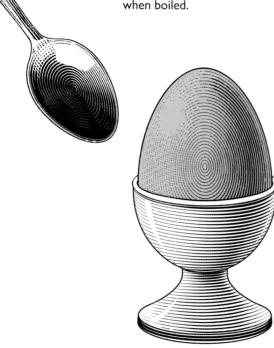

QUIZ
SCIENCE

Ready to win first prize at the science fair? Sort your protons from your electrons, don your lab coat, and prepare to unleash your inner genius.

QUESTIONS:

1. The Maillard reaction makes food turn what color when you cook it?

2. The Dead Sea is not a sea but a lake. True or false?

3. Does the production of chlorophyll in leaves speed up or slow down in the winter?

4. What are the five tastes you can experience with your tongue?

5. Yawning increases the levels of oxygen in the blood—true or false?

6. Which is more harmful to dogs: dark chocolate, milk chocolate, or white chocolate?

7. Which dictatorial regime experimented with substance N in the 1930s?

8. Is the periodic table complete?

9. What is the name of India's "twin town"?

10. Luminol spray shows crime scene investigators where ketchup has been—true or false?

Turn to page 248 for the answers.

FILM AND THEATER

113 WHO ARE THE BEST-PAID PETS IN CINEMA HISTORY?

Dogs are easy to train, eager to please, and adorable to boot, so unsurprisingly, man's best friend has featured in movies since filmmaking began. And while most pooches pick up only a few hundred bucks a day for being on set, one of cinema's earliest stars earned more than many of her human colleagues.

THERE'S NO PLACE LIKE BONE

Terry, the cairn terrier who played Toto in 1939's *The Wizard of Oz* alongside Judy Garland, was paid $125 per week to play Dorothy's loyal pet. The actors who played the Munchkins, however, were on about $50 per week. Adjusted for inflation, Terry was earning about $2,200 per week—more than many Americans at that time. She also starred with Shirley Temple in *Bright Eyes* and went on to feature in *The Women* with Joan Crawford.

MONEYED MUTTS

Terry was by no means Hollywood's most well-paid acting dog. Jack Russell terrier Moose appeared in one feature film, as the titular character in *My Dog Skip*, but he made most of his cash from his ten-year role as Marty Crane's dog, Eddie, in the long-running TV comedy series *Frasier*. He relinquished the part to his son, Enzo, when he retired. He reportedly earned about $10,000 per episode and featured in nearly 200 episodes of the show's 11-year run. But $2 million is peanuts compared to the amount Rin Tin Tin made from his Warner Bros. contract in the 1930s. The Alsatian was a superstar in his own right, with a private chef and his own radio show. He earned $6,000 per week at the height of his popularity, starring in 28 adventure films such as *The Lightning Warrior* and *The Lone Defender*. In today's money, that's around $87,000 per week!

BAD MOOD, BIG CHECK

Grumpy Cat, otherwise known as Tardar Sauce, is one of a whole new breed of four-legged fortune-makers. Social media sites and YouTube have spawned an entire industry of furry stars posing and purring for big bucks. Grumpy Cat, who even has her own agent, reportedly earned her owner close to $100 million in two years, including the earnings from her film debut, *Grumpy Cat's Worst Christmas Ever*. Not bad for a kitty whose main talent is looking miserable.

BIG AT THE BOX OFFICE

Cats and dogs aren't the only non-human performers to bring in the big bucks. Over the years, filmmakers have paid big money for some truly massive stars, including Bart the Kodiak bear, who appeared alongside Brad Pitt in *Legends of the Fall* and Anthony Hopkins in *The Edge*— performances that earned him $6 million. Bart was born into captivity and when just five weeks old was adopted by his trainers. He grew to 9 feet 6 inches tall and weighed in at 1,480 pounds.

114 WHY ARE ALL KABUKI ACTORS MEN?

Kabuki is a traditional Japanese performance art. It dates from the early 17th century, and is believed to have originated with the performances of a female dancer—which is strange, seeing as all the contemporary performers are men.

SEX ON THE STAGE

The word *kabuki* comes from *kabukimono*—a word used to describe people who dressed in extreme clothing and did shocking or unspeakable things. In modern Japanese, the word's three characters mean "song," "dance," and "skill." The first historical reference to Kabuki can be linked to a woman named Izumo no Okuni. While not a lot is known about her, she is credited with inventing a dance called *kabuki odori* with a troupe of other women performers. As it became more popular, it developed into a brash and vulgar art form and inevitably, sex workers performed too. Soon the art form became too controversial for the Japanese government; in 1629 they banned women from performing in them. Teenage boys (*wakashu*) took up women's places in what was then known as *wakashu kabuki*, but by 1652, the government had outlawed them too; it was a ban that took over a decade to come into effect, due to Kabuki's popularity. The ban did not last long, and since then, men have played all the characters.

IT'S SHOWTIME

In 2005, Kabuki was recognized by UNESCO as a Masterpiece of the Oral and Intangible Heritage of Humanity, joining practices from around the world with important cultural and historical significance. There are two main types of Kabuki—*kyogen* and *buyo*. The former is more akin to a play, with the story based on historical events or a fictional tale. The latter is more of a dance performance. Unlike traditional Western theater, Kabuki bears some resemblance to British pantomime, where the actors and the audience interact throughout the show. Audience members are known to call out actors' names and clap along, and the actors regularly perform among the audience. Originally, Kabuki shows would run throughout the day, so spectators might watch only a portion of the program.

FIVE QUICK FACTS

 1

THE 1976 FILM *THE OMEN* WAS CURSED

While filming the classic horror, the special effects designer died in a car crash, his girlfriend was decapitated, an animal handler was killed by a tiger, and lightning struck planes carrying the cast and crew.

 2

THE SNOW IN *THE WIZARD OF OZ* WAS A HEALTH HAZARD

In the classic film's famous poppy-field scene, the snow falling on Dorothy and her new friends was actually asbestos-based fake snow—a popular decoration at the time.

 3

IN CHINESE OPERA, THE COLOR OF A CHARACTER'S MASK HAS MEANING

The dominant color gives the audience a clue about their personality—for example, red means prosperous, loyal, and heroic; yellow means ambitious and intelligent; while silver is reserved for a god or demon.

 4

PSYCHO WAS THE FIRST MOVIE TO SHOW A TOILET FLUSHING

In 1960 it was considered inappropriate to see a toilet on screen, so director Alfred Hitchcock had a shot of a piece of paper failing to flush down the loo for some extra shock factor. Oh my!

 5

WAYANG KULIT FANS HAVE STAMINA

Indonesian puppet theater, or *Wayang Kulit*, dates back to the first century AD. The puppets are made from buffalo hides mounted on bamboo sticks, with performances often lasting for a whole night.

115 WHICH WAS SHAKESPEARE'S MOST SUCCESSFUL PLAY IN HIS LIFETIME?

In England, prior to 1576, actors performed in college halls, private houses, and inns, but the construction of theaters such as the Rose and the Globe—where William Shakespeare himself owned shares—provided dedicated spaces where up to 3,000 people could watch a production together.

HISTORY BUFFS

Unlike today, when *A Midsummer Night's Dream*, *Hamlet*, *Macbeth*, and *Romeo and Juliet* top lists of the most performed and most popular Shakespeare plays, it was his history plays that were the most sought after in his own lifetime. The two most-published plays between the 1590s and 1630s were *Henry IV Part I*, published 11 times, and *Richard III*, published 10 times. Shakespeare was writing about powerful historical figures and events not long in the past. Richard III, for example, died in 1485, heralding the end of the Wars of the Roses and the start of the mighty Tudor dynasty. His historical figures included Queen Elizabeth I, one of Shakespeare's chief patrons. Being a Shakespeare history fan in the 16th and 17th centuries was not too dissimilar from modern audiences being enthralled by dramas set in World War I or the reign of Queen Victoria.

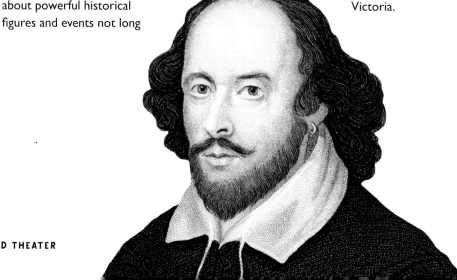

Modern audiences are less likely to know the difference between their Henrys, while "To be or not to be," uttered by a fictional Danish prince, has become the best-known line of Shakespeare's work. Over four hundred years after Shakespeare's death, *Hamlet* has been translated into more than 75 languages, even *Star Trek*'s Klingon.

CHEAP AS BEER

Plays were performed most afternoons, meaning up to 20,000 people a week paid to go and see a show (a huge number when you consider the population of London was around 250,000). As a result, plays only had very short runs and were quickly replaced, meaning it was hard for anything to be a runaway hit like today's Broadway blockbusters. That said, while nothing was technically a "box office" smash, the term is derived from the box that audiences had to deposit their money into when they entered the theater or sometimes to get to the good seats. And the theater wasn't just for the rich—you could watch a show for just one "penny," although you'd have to stand in the open-air "yard" area that surrounded the stage. If you think a penny doesn't sound like much, you'd be right. For the same price you could buy a loaf of bread or two-thirds of a gallon of beer.

GLOBAL FAILURE

While his audiences were big fans of his ten history plays, Shakespeare might have had a less favorable response after one particular performance of his last, *Henry VIII*. During a 1613 production, the Globe Theatre came to an untimely end when a stage cannon ignited the thatched roof, burning the whole building to the ground.

WHICH COUNTRY PRODUCES THE MOST MOVIES EACH YEAR?

In the Western world, people associate the film industry with Hollywood—America's movie-producing powerhouse. But while it's true that the United States rakes in around 25 percent of the world's total box office revenue, that is not were the most films are being produced.

BOLLYWOOD BOOM

India's Bollywood film industry is worth closer to the $2 billion mark but blows the competition out of the water when it comes to making movies. Each year, between 1,500 and 2,000 are produced by the nation's studios, compared to a paltry 786 released by American producers in 2019. And Nigeria's Nollywood, where approximately 2,500 films are made each year, is hot on India's tail. Many of these movies aren't released theatrically, but they still contribute to an industry that's estimated to bring in between $500 million and $1 billion each year.

ONCE AGAIN FOR THE CHEAP SEATS

So why the difference in revenue? Firstly, there's only one cinema screen per 96,300 people in India, compared to one per 7,800 in the United States. Secondly, while millions of cinema tickets are sold in India, they cost a lot less than in the United States, so the industry makes less money. In 2019, Indians bought 1.03 billion cinema tickets—not too far off the 1.2 billion tickets sold in the United States. But domestic box office takings in India were $1.5 billion compared to $11.2 billion in the United States. And when it comes to exports, America dominates: almost 75 percent of Hollywood's revenue comes from other countries. Meanwhile, India produces films in over 40 regional languages, meaning more niche audiences, costlier production, and fewer nationwide blockbusters.

117 WAS THERE REALLY A PHANTOM AT THE OPERA IN PARIS?

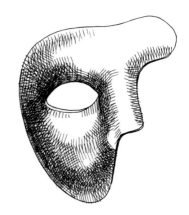

Andrew Lloyd Webber's musical *The Phantom of the Opera* is based on a work by Parisian novelist Gaston Leroux. It begins with the line "The Opera ghost really existed." Leroux later claimed that the theatrical ghoul was real, and while this has never been proven, the spooky story does have roots in reality.

MURKY DEPTHS

Leroux's 1910 Gothic romance, set in the Palais Garnier in Paris, refers to a lake in the building's bowels, beneath the cellars where Erik, the phantom, lives. This creepy "lake" actually exists. When trying to lay concrete foundations in 1861, it came to light that the building would be set above an arm of the river Seine. After trying and failing to pump the site dry, a large stone water tank was created, covered by a small grate. The pressure prevents any more water from rising up through the foundations, and the tank helps to stabilize the building.

DEATH BY CHANDELIER

Before becoming a celebrated crime writer, Leroux worked at *Le Matin* as a courtroom reporter. On May 21, 1896, one of the newspaper's headlines read "Five hundred kilos on a concierge's head." It referred to an incident the previous evening at the Palais Garnier, where one woman had died and two had been injured after electrical faults caused an 800-pound counterweight to fall from the chandelier above the audience during a performance. In the novel's climax, Erik causes a chandelier to fall into the stalls as a distraction so that he can kidnap Christine, the opera-singing heroine.

WHO WAS THE WORLD'S FIRST ACTOR?

The word "thespian" has been used in English to describe actors since the late 17th century. Its origins lie in ancient Greece, where in 534 BC, a poet named Thespis of Icaria stepped forward to recite the lines of the character Dionysus. In doing so, he became the world's first official actor.

THE CHORUS LINE

Thespis was performing as the leader of a Greek chorus—a group of between 12 and 50 performers who would perform choral hymns, called dithyrambs, dressed in costumes and masks. This particular performance was thought to be part of the City Dionysia, a spring festival in Athens in honor of Dionysus, the god of wine, fertility, and theater. The procession involved a statue of the god being carried through the streets to a temple at the foot of the Acropolis, as well as sacrificial bulls, and lots of wine. The festival also featured competitions in music, singing, poetry, and dance, and Thespis is believed to have been one of the victors.

STANDING OUT FROM THE CROWD

There is disagreement among scholars about Thespis's involvement in the development of Greek drama, but some believe he was the first to incorporate speeches into choral tragedy performances, with the introduction of a prologue and monologues, changing the face of theater forever. His other revolutionary step was to be the first person to appear on stage as a character rather than himself, when he spoke for Dionysus.

119 WHY DID FILMMAKERS ASK BRUCE LEE TO PUNCH MORE SLOWLY?

Bruce Lee's first major role was as the sidekick Kato on the TV series *The Green Hornet*. His martial arts skills, displayed at Long Beach's International Karate Championships in 1964, had impressed producers—but it clearly hadn't occurred to them that Lee was too fast to capture on film.

PACY PUNCHING

Original footage of Bruce Lee's full-throttle moves as Kato made it look like he was standing still while his opponents dropped like flies around him—his punches were too fast to be picked up by the cameras of the time. Lee was asked to slow down so the blur of his fist could be captured on film, then the footage was slowed down further in the edit so the audience could perceive the punches. That's how fast he was! Lee went on to star in a few films showcasing his martial arts skills, including *The Way of the Dragon* (1972) and *Enter the Dragon* (1973).

THE COIN TRICKSTER

Lee's speed is legendary—even more so because he died at 32, before his acting career really had the chance to take off. One party trick he was known for was grabbing a coin out of your hand so fast you barely knew it had happened. Standing a few feet away, he'd tell an unsuspecting volunteer to close their fist around the coin in their palm as soon as they saw him move. They would, only to look down and see their coin replaced with another and a smug Lee, holding theirs, back in his starting spot.

120 WHO BUILT THE HOLLYWOOD SIGN?

The Hollywood sign, recognized the world over, has become synonymous with Los Angeles's prolific film industry. But when it was originally constructed in 1923, it was as a rather expensive advertisement for a new real-estate development called Hollywoodland. The original 45-foot-high sign included "land" at the end and was illuminated by 4,000 lightbulbs.

SCALING UP

Los Angeles Times publisher Harry Chandler's upscale real-estate development advertisement cost him and his partners $21,000 (equivalent to $300,000 today). Tinseltown was booming, and he wanted in on the real-estate gold mine. The flashing sign, which mules hauled up the side of the mountain, might have been a big gamble, but it paid off. When the development opened, Chandler's newspaper declared it the first hillside residential development in the United States, and ads warned people of the "ever-present danger to the children of big cities" and urged them to "Come to Hollywoodland." Immediately, 120 buyers signed contracts—but the dream was not to be. When the Great Depression struck at the end of the 1920s, the partners' other investments took a hit, and construction on the development was abruptly halted.

A NIP AND A TUCK

Like many of Hollywood's stars, the Hollywood sign has had a few facelifts over the years. Only ever intended to last for 18 months, the original sign was constructed from 3-foot by 9-foot metal panels, held together by scaffolding built from telephone poles, wires, and pipes. As a result of the sign's temporary nature, it needed constant maintenance, which stopped around the time the Hollywoodland dream collapsed during the Depression; for a while, the sign read "Ollywoodland" after the H toppled over. In 1949, the Hollywood Chamber of Commerce stepped in to restore the whole sign, with the exception of the last four letters.

CELEBRITY SAVIORS

Hollywood celebrities have taken it upon themselves to keep the sign in good condition. A 1978 alliance, which included Alice Cooper, Andy Williams, and *Playboy* founder Hugh Hefner, saw the stars pledge $28,000 each to fund a replacement. There was a three-month period without a sign, while it was replaced with a more structurally sound version with steel footings. The land it stands on is now owned by the City of Los Angeles after it was purchased in 2010 by another alliance of famous faces and brands, including Tom Hanks, Norman Lear, and the Walt Disney Company. For the pricey sum of $12.5 million, the land surrounding the sign is now safe from development—ironically, the very thing it was originally advertising.

THE BIRTH OF AN INDUSTRY

Hollywood was founded as a California district in 1887. The origins of the name are not certain, but it's thought that one of the district's founders met a woman on the train whose summer home had that name, or that it was a reference to the area's red-berried toyon shrub, also known as California holly. In 1910—a year before the first film studio opened there—Hollywood merged with Los Angeles.

121 WHY DID JOSEPHINE BAKER HIDE MESSAGES IN HER SHEET MUSIC?

She was a star of stage and screen, and a pioneering performer and civil rights activist who paved the way for other black artists, but the enigmatic Josephine Baker was something else too: a spy.

A STAR IS BORN

Born and raised in St. Louis, Missouri, in 1906, faced with the atrocities and prejudices of the Jim Crow era, Baker worked as a domestic servant as a child before running away from home. By 15, her talent and charisma had meant a move to New York City, where she danced in the chorus line of Broadway shows, but it was in Paris where she found her most loyal audience. She was a sensation, performing at the Folies Bergère and socializing with the artistic elite, including Ernest Hemingway, Pablo Picasso, and Jean Cocteau. In 1937, not long before war broke out, she became a French citizen.

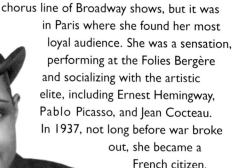

THE SPY WHO SANG

Her love and devotion to her adopted country extended far beyond wielding a passport, however. She was recruited by French military intelligence as a spy, using her performance schedule as the perfect cover to gather information. Wherever she went she was invited to glamorous embassy parties, where she eavesdropped on Italian, Japanese, and German officials to find out the movements of German troops. Together with her "assistant," fellow spy Jacques Abtey, they recorded this information using invisible ink on her sheet music. She is also reported to have pinned important photos to her underwear in case her luggage was ever searched. After the war, she received the Croix de Guerre and Legion of Honour from General Charles de Gaulle himself for her efforts.

QUIZ
FILM AND THEATER

There's no business like show business! And there's nothing people love more than an entertainment buff. Here's your chance to prove you're a star.

QUESTIONS:

1. The dog playing Toto in *The Wizard of Oz* was paid more than Judy Garland—true or false?

2. Since 1652, who has performed traditional Japanese Kabuki?

3. During a production of which play did the original Globe Theatre burn to the ground: *Henry VIII*, *Mamma Mia!*, or *Cats*?

4. *The Phantom of the Opera* is set in the opera house of which European city?

5. What is Nigeria's film industry known as?

6. Complete the title of this famous Bruce Lee film: *Enter the_____*.

7. The Hollywood sign was originally advertising a real-estate development—true or false?

8. What was Thespis of Icaria the first person to do?

9. Josephine Baker was born in France. True or false?

10. *Hamlet* has been translated into *Star Trek*'s Klingon language—true or false?

Turn to page 249 for the answers.

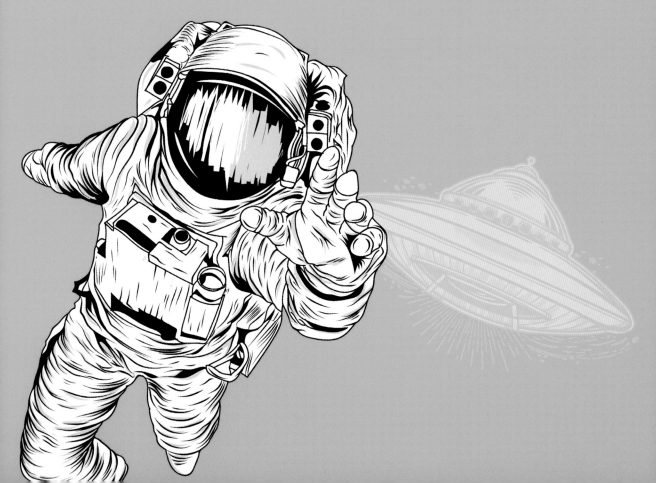

THE UNIVERSE
AND SPACE

122 WOULD LIFE ON EARTH BE BETTER WITHOUT THE MOON?

The Moon is currently moving away from Earth at a rate of 1.5 inches a year as its orbit gets bigger. That's the same speed at which your fingernails grow. But if things sped up to the point that the Moon was no longer around, what would life on Earth be like?

CHANGING TIDES

The Moon is kept in our orbit because of the gravitational force that Earth is exerting on it, and the Moon exerts a gravitational force on Earth, which is responsible for our changing tides. There is more gravitational pull on the side of Earth that is facing the Moon than on the center of the planet and the side facing away from it. This causes the oceans' water to stretch outward on either side, which is known as "tidal bulge." As Earth rotates throughout the day, the pull causes high tides twice a day, followed by low tides six hours later. Without the Moon there would still be tides, because the Sun has an effect too, but they would be less extreme. The tides are important—they help move heat from the equator to the poles, bringing cyclical warm and cool temperatures. Species rely on these temperatures for migration, and their predictability is useful to fishers, military vessels, and even surfers.

IS IT BEDTIME YET?

As Earth rotates, it drags the position of these tidal bulges ahead of where they otherwise would be, directly under the Moon. The counteracting effect of the Moon on these tidal bulges results in friction that slows down Earth's rotation and pushes the Moon farther away, increasing its orbit. When the Moon was first formed, days on Earth were only five hours long, but as the Moon has gradually moved away from our planet, this braking effect has increased a day's length to the current 24 hours. If this process were to speed up, with the Moon disappearing into the distance, our days would get longer and longer. However, if we'd never had the Moon to begin with, we'd barely have time to get up and get to work before it was bedtime again.

WOBBLY PLANET

One benefit of having the Moon around is that it prevents Earth from wobbling while it spins. The Moon acts as a stabilizer, keeping Earth angled on its axis at a tilt of 23 degrees. Because of this tilt, the Northern Hemisphere gets longer days and warmer weather during its summer, when it's tilted closer to the Sun. Without the Moon, Earth would be unstable and parts of the world would have to deal with more extreme temperature swings than we're currently used to.

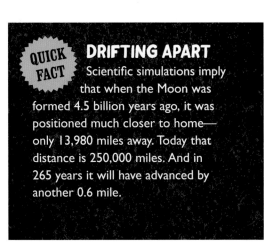

QUICK FACT

DRIFTING APART

Scientific simulations imply that when the Moon was formed 4.5 billion years ago, it was positioned much closer to home—only 13,980 miles away. Today that distance is 250,000 miles. And in 265 years it will have advanced by another 0.6 mile.

123 WHAT HAPPENED TO THE SOVIET SPACE DOGS?

Between 1951 and 1966, the Soviets pulled ahead in the Space Race after betting their money on dogs to pave the way for humans. While over a dozen dogs didn't survive to wag their tails another day, those that did became Soviet heroes for their service to space exploration.

WHY DOGS?

Before the days of manned space travel and the International Space Station, both American and Soviet space agencies relied on animals to test the limits of what was possible. The Americans sent monkeys and chimpanzees up to the stars, but the Soviets decided dogs were calmer and would be better able to handle the stress than other animals. Monkeys, they thought, were more likely to succumb to disease. Rather than breed dogs specifically for the purpose, or source pedigree champions, they decided street mutts, adept at handling Moscow's extreme winters and accustomed to hunger, would be most capable of handling the pressures of space travel. Canine candidates had to be between 13 and 16 pounds, aged between one and a half and six, female (because it would be easier for them to urinate in the small capsules), and with light-colored fur so they would show up on cameras.

THE FIRST DOGS IN SPACE

On August 15, 1951, two dogs, Dezik and Tsygan, became the first mammals to successfully survive a suborbital flight. They reached a height of 63 miles before their rocket's nose cone parachuted them safely back to Earth. Traveling at a speed of 2,600 miles per hour apparently had no lasting adverse effects on the dogs, which were wagging their tails when they were released from the capsule. The two dogs were part

of a nine-strong pack put through the training program to prepare for the flight. Dezik was back up a week later with another dog called Lisa; unfortunately, the rocket's parachute failed to open and both dogs died. Launch security officer Anatoly Blagon didn't want Tsygan to face the same fate, so he adopted her and took her home with him to Moscow, where she lived a long life.

SOVIET HEROES

The first dog in orbit was Laika—she was sent up with the second Soviet satellite, *Sputnik 2*, in 1957. While for years it was thought Laika survived up to seven days in space, in 2002 it was revealed that she had actually died within a few hours of the launch due to a thermal conductivity miscalculation. No recovery system was put in place for Laika's mission, meaning she was seen around the world as a victim of the Space Race.

Laika's achievements were soon eclipsed in 1960 by Belka and Strelka, the first animals to be recovered successfully from orbit. They were international celebrities, appearing on television, meeting important politicians, and becoming the faces of Soviet space travel. One of Strelka's puppies, Pushinka, was even given as a present to President John F. Kennedy's daughter, although not before the Secret Service had examined the pup for bugging devices.

124 HOW BIG IS THE MILKY WAY?

Our solar system—made up of the Sun, eight planets, dwarf planets, and natural satellites such as our Moon—is located in an outer spiral arm of the Milky Way galaxy. Neptune, the farthest planet from our Sun, is located nearly 2.7 billion miles from Earth. And beyond *our* solar system is the rest of the galaxy.

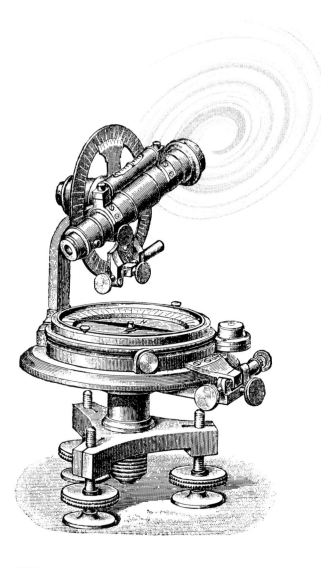

BIG BLACK HOLE

There are four major arms to the Milky Way, and they're made up of at least 100 billion stars. The distance across the galaxy is about 100,000 light-years. It's hard to fathom how far that is, but one light-year is approximately 5.6 trillion miles. In the center is a massive black hole, estimated to be about 4 million times bigger than our Sun. Our solar system, along with all the other stars, is orbiting around that black hole, traveling at speeds of 515,000 miles per hour. But it's so huge that it takes 230 million years to get all the way around.

KEEP IT LOCAL

Parts of our galaxy are believed to be around 13.5 billion years old, which is only a few hundred million years younger than the universe itself. It is part of a collection of 30 galaxies known as the Local Group. The largest member is the Andromeda galaxy, and the Milky Way is the second largest. The Local Group is just one of many galaxy clusters that are moving away from each other as the universe expands.

125 WHY DON'T WE FEEL THE EARTH MOVING?

Unless you live near the poles, where things turn slightly slower, you're currently sitting atop a giant rock spinning on its axis at a constant speed of 1,040 miles per hour (1,525 feet per second). But because planet Earth is so darn big, you don't feel a thing.

HEAD IN THE CLOUDS

Because Earth's atmosphere is moving at the same speed you are, you don't feel the speed the planet is traveling at. Being on Earth is a bit like traveling on a plane, but twice as fast. Because a plane is traveling so quickly, when it's not speeding up or slowing down you can close your eyes and barely perceive the fact you're moving at 500 miles per hour. The only way you can really tell is by looking outside and seeing the clouds.

PREPARE FOR LANDING

Beyond Earth's rotating atmosphere are the Moon, Sun, and stars, which all give us an indication that we're moving. But because we're so far from them, and the change is slow, constant, and gradual, it almost looks like they're moving and we're constant, which is what our ancestors thought. If Earth were to suddenly speed up or slow down, like a plane coming in to land, you'd be sure to feel it. It's unlikely, though. For our planet to stop rotating or to rotate at a different speed, it would have to be unbalanced by an unimaginable external force—a collision on an interplanetary scale.

126 WHAT ARE THE CHANCES OF GETTING HIT BY A METEOR?

A meteor is the spectacular streak of light you see trailing behind a meteoroid as it enters Earth's atmosphere. If a meteoroid crash-lands on Earth, it becomes a meteorite. Thus, the chances of getting hit by a meteor are none, but there's a minuscule chance that a meteorite could get you.

SLIM CHANCE

A meteoroid is a small interplanetary object usually consisting of particles that have broken off from asteroids or comets. Each day, about 4 billion meteoroids enter the Earth's atmosphere, but they generally vaporize before they reach the surface. It's rare that anything much bigger manages to get through. Some larger asteroids do make it, with a 1985 study calculating that the rate at which humans are hit by meteorites is 0.0055 per year, or one event every 180 years.

BRUISED BY A METEORITE

This particularly rare honor, if you can call it that, was bestowed upon Ann Hodges in 1954. While she napped on her couch in Sylacauga, Alabama, an 8-pound meteorite about the size of a softball crashed through the ceiling, bounced off a radio, and hit her on the hip. Other than the shock and a large round bruise, she was unharmed. Ann hoped to sell the meteorite for a small fortune, but after big offers weren't forthcoming, she donated it to the Alabama Museum of Natural History, where it still resides.

HOT ROCKS

Latest research suggests between 100 and 2,000 meteorites land on Earth each year. If you're lucky enough to find one, you might be able to make a few bucks. Space rocks tend to go for around $2 per gram—they're worth even more if someone saw them fall. The Holy Grail is a bit of the Moon or Mars, which can fetch up to $1,000 per gram. But you might need to pack your bags and head to Antarctica or North Africa to find them, because these reddish rocks are much easier to spot on ice or sand dunes.

FIVE QUICK FACTS

1 **MOST OF THE UNIVERSE IS INVISIBLE**

Because 96 percent of the universe is made up of dark energy and matter, comprising particles that don't interact with regular matter or light, we're unable to see most of it.

2 **YOU CAN'T BURP IN SPACE**

When you burp on Earth, gravity keeps down the solids and liquids from the food you just ate, but without gravity, it's not only the gas that escapes, so burping is essentially puking.

3 **IT MIGHT RAIN DIAMONDS ON SATURN**

The high-pressure atmosphere on Saturn, as well as Neptune, Uranus, and Jupiter, could very well crystallize carbon atoms, turning them into diamonds. Scientists have speculated that it might rain up to 2.2 million pounds of diamonds on Saturn every year.

4 **BACON WAS THE FIRST THING EATEN ON THE MOON**

Bacon was on the menu for the first scheduled meal Neil Armstrong and Buzz Aldrin tucked into in 1969. It was enjoyed with peaches, sugar cookie cubes, pineapple grapefruit drink, and coffee.

5 **METAL CAN STICK TOGETHER IN A VACUUM**

Cold welding refers to when two pieces of the same type of metal touch in the vacuum of space and then permanently bond together. It happens because unlike on Earth, where air and water separate them, the atoms of the two pieces have no way of knowing that they are different.

127 WHO STOLE EINSTEIN'S BRAIN?

After eminent physicist Albert Einstein died of a ruptured aneurysm in the early hours of April 18, 1955, his body wound up in the morgue at Princeton Hospital in New Jersey. Presiding over the autopsy was the on-call pathologist, Thomas Stoltz Harvey, who would become known as the man who stole Einstein's brain.

WAS IT REALLY THEFT?

The jury will probably always be out over whether Einstein wanted his brain to be studied. Some have reported that he left strict instructions for his remains to be cremated and his ashes scattered in secret, to avoid a grave site becoming a shrine to him and his work. But others, notably Ronald Clark in his 1984 biography, have written that Einstein insisted his brain should be used for research.

Rather than simply identify and confirm the cause of death, Harvey sawed open Einstein's skull and removed his brain. He also removed his eyes and gave them to the physicist's eye doctor. The family's permission was not sought until after Harvey had taken ownership of the organ; Einstein's son, Hans Albert, was furious when he learned his father's dying wishes had not been met, but was convinced by Harvey to grant permission, in the hope his father's brain would reveal the very nature of genius.

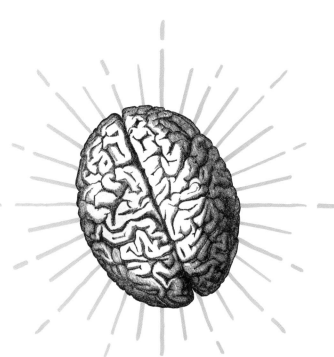

PRESERVING GENIUS

After the autopsy, Harvey weighed and measured this "genius" brain. It weighed 2.64 pounds, toward the lower end of the normal range for a man of 76. He then took the brain to a laboratory at the University of Pennsylvania, where a rare instrument, called a microtone, was used to divide the brain into microscopic sections, which were embedded in celloidin—a chemical that hardens tissue. There were believed to be 240 pieces in total. Many of these slides were sent to the leading neuropathologists of the day, but none of them found anything notable about the brain, and their findings were never published.

RETURNING THE RELIC

After effectively stealing Einstein's brain, Harvey's career never recovered. He lost his job at Princeton Hospital and then lost his medical license in the late 1980s for failing a competency examination. He ended up working on the assembly line at a plastic extrusion factory, and died in 2007. A 1978 interview with Harvey renewed interest in the scientist's brain, and a number of studies were conducted, with inconclusive results. In 1998, Harvey handed over the remaining 170 pieces of Einstein's brain in his possession to the chief pathologist at the University Medical Center of Princeton—the contemporary name for Princeton Hospital.

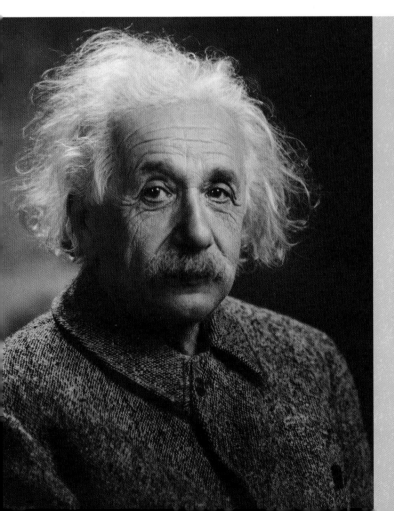

PRECIOUS EYES

Einstein's eyes are believed to be peering into the darkness of a New Jersey safe-deposit box. Einstein's ophthalmologist, Henry Abrams, remained the owner of the eyes for the rest of his life—he died in 2009, aged 97. In a 1994 interview, he denied the eyes would go up for auction, saying: "Having his eyes means the professor's life has not ended. A part of him is still with me." They've still not been sold publicly.

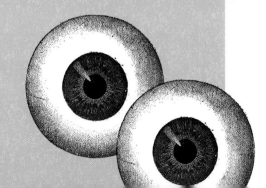

WHAT'S ON THE FAR SIDE OF THE MOON?

When the Soviet *Luna 3* spacecraft captured the far side of the Moon on camera for the first time in 1959, the result was shocking. There might not have been little green men hiding out there, but the landscape was markedly different from the side we'd all been staring at for millennia.

FAR, FAR AWAY

The Moon is tidally locked in place, meaning the same side always faces Earth. The first humans to see the surface with their own eyes were the crew of *Apollo 8*, who orbited the Moon in 1968. While the near side has huge regions of ancient lava flows, called maria, caused by volcanic activity, the far side is littered with crater impacts; the crust is thicker, making it more difficult for magma to erupt on the surface, creating a completely different appearance.

BEWARE OF THE DARK SIDE

Many people mistake the "far side" of the Moon for the "dark side," probably because of Pink Floyd's hugely successful 1973 album entitled *The Dark Side of the Moon*. There is a dark side of the Moon, as the Moon, like Earth, has daytime and nighttime. However, as on Earth, that "side" is constantly changing. If you were able to set up camp on the far side of the Moon, you'd experience both day and night. But because it takes the Moon around 29 Earth days to complete one full rotation on its axis around the Sun, as well as a complete orbit around Earth, you would experience two weeks of daytime, then two weeks of nighttime.

129 DOES SPACE NEED CLEANING?

Space is a very messy place. There are over 500,000 pieces of debris orbiting Earth at any given time, some 20,000 times larger than a softball. This space trash can travel at speeds up to 17,500 miles per hour, and even a tiny piece can cause major damage to a satellite or spacecraft.

MAN-MADE MESS

There are two types of space debris—natural meteoroids, orbiting the Sun, and particles from man-made objects, orbiting Earth and known as "orbital debris." The latter is made up of larger items like nonfunctional spacecraft and abandoned launch vehicle components. With over 1,000 operational satellites orbiting Earth, it's important that this debris is monitored and that future waste is minimized as much as possible.

CLEANING IT UP

In 1995, NASA issued a set of guidelines for the mitigation of orbital debris. As well as preventing the creation of new debris, their measures involve designing satellites that can withstand the impact of small debris, and maneuvering spacecraft and satellites where necessary to avoid major collisions. Another tactic is controlled reentry, where a more accurate landing position can be calculated over an uninhabited area, such as the ocean, for any bits of debris that don't

decay on reentry. The year 2017 also saw the launch of RemoveDEBRIS, a multimillion-dollar mission funded by the European Commission and led by the Surrey Space Centre in the UK, to test a range of space-cleaning devices. In the first mission of its kind, a platform of harpoon, net, and sail devices was launched into space and tested using artificial trash.

130 WHY HAVEN'T WE MET ANY ALIENS?

Maybe we've just not been looking hard enough. Our Sun is one of up to 400 billion stars in the Milky Way, one of the universe's 100 billion galaxies. If all those stars have on average one planet orbiting them, that's an awful lot of space for us mere mortals to scope out.

THE GREAT SILENCE

A 2013 study used data from the Kepler space telescope to assert that one in five Sun-like stars has an Earth-sized planet orbiting in the habitable region, where liquid water is possible, allowing life to flourish. The fact that we've yet to find evidence of extraterrestrial civilization in our galaxy or beyond, given how likely it is that it exists, poses the question: Why haven't aliens visited our planet yet? This has become known as the Fermi paradox: "the great silence."

FILTERED OUT

One possible explanation for the Fermi paradox is the "great filter" hypothesis. This suggests that an obstacle stands in the way of ordinary dead matter becoming "advanced exploding lasting life" and prevents other life-forms from developing enough to reach us. The theory also suggests that the "great filter" could still be ahead of planet Earth, and without proof that we've already overcome it—such as through the emergence of reproductive molecules or simple single-celled life in our planet's ancient history—we must assume some great catastrophe lies in wait for us.

TOO FAR APART

Another suggestion is that while there might be other intelligent life out there, we're just too far apart to communicate. However, another life-form might pick up on a message we've sent, even if they can't reply. With this in mind, in 1974 a transmission known as the "Arecibo message" was sent using a radio telescope to the Hercules Globular Cluster of about 300,000 stars. It contained 1,679 binary digits that communicated, among other things, the numbers one to ten, the population of Earth, and a graphic of the double helix structure of DNA. The message was sent only once—symbolically, to show it could be done—and we've yet to hear anything back.

BREAKTHROUGH THE SILENCE

Our extraterrestrial treasure hunt has so far been fairly limited—the Hubble Telescope has performed only one atmospheric study of an Earth-sized planet. But in 2015 a $100 million project called Breakthrough Listen launched a plan to change that by carrying out a survey of the closest million stars, our galaxy, and the 100 nearest galaxies. This comprehensive study, expected to take ten years, hopes to find a definitive answer to the Fermi paradox, using powerful radio telescopes for signals.

WHOSE PARADOX?

Enrico Fermi raised the idea of the great silence in 1950, and it has troubled scientists ever since. Fermi won the Nobel Prize in Physics for his work in radioactivity. He'd left Italy for a new life in America and went on to build a prototype for a nuclear reactor. He also worked on the Manhattan Project to develop the first atomic bomb.

DO ASTRONAUTS EAT THEIR VEGGIES?

In 1961, Soviet cosmonaut Gherman Titov became the first human to consume food in space, followed in 1962 by the first American, John Glenn. Titov tucked into soup, liver food paste, and black currant juice, while Glenn ate applesauce through a squeeze tube. But today's astronauts do a little better than that.

COSMIC DINING

With over half a century of space exploration and scientific development, eating in space has improved significantly since the 1960s. Astronauts make their menu choices preflight from a wide variety of options, many containing fruit and vegetables. However, most meals consist of rehydratable food and/or thermostabilized food, heat-treated to destroy any potentially harmful microorganisms. Rehydratable food is ideal for space travel as it's lighter, takes up less space, and the water needed to prepare it is available in abundance—it was a by-product of an engine's fuel cells.

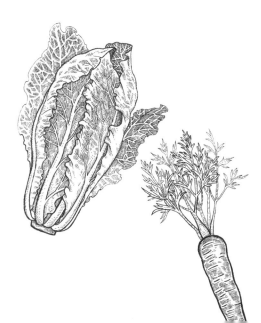

The first apples, bananas, and carrot and celery sticks were flown on the space shuttle in 1983, and since then fresh fruit and vegetables are always included. Fresh produce is also taken to the International Space Station (ISS) via resupply cargo vehicles, but must be consumed within a few days due to the lack of refrigeration on board.

VEG-01

In 2015, Expedition 44 crew members on board the ISS ate the first space-grown food as part of an experiment known as Veg-01. Nicknamed "Veggie" by NASA, the result of years of work was a red romaine lettuce, and according to astronaut Scott Kelly, it tasted "good. Kinda like arugula."

The Veggie system, about the size of a stovetop, uses red and blue LEDs—which emit the most light—to stimulate plant growth. But for the lettuce, green LEDs were added, to make the plant more recognizable and therefore more appetizing. The seeds are activated in rooting "pillows"—chambers consisting of clay, fertilizer, and water—and the lettuce was ready for harvest after about a month. It wasn't the first lettuce grown in space; its predecessor was also a horticultural success, but was flown back to Earth for testing, rather than risk any contamination by the astronauts.

In 2016, the first flower to be grown successfully in space—a zinnia, part of the daisy family—bloomed for the first time on the ISS. This was followed in 2018 with a gardening experiment whereby NASA irradiated tomato seeds to be grown in low Earth orbit.

THE BENEFITS OF SPACE GARDENING

The ISS has nowhere near enough space to facilitate a large-scale garden, but the experiments taking place there are the first steps toward making space missions more sustainable. Spaceflights are restricted by the amount of supplies that can be carried on board, or must rely on being resupplied. But if astronauts were able to grow some of their own food, they could travel for longer, exploring deeper into space. It's also believed that growing fresh food has a positive impact on the astronauts' state of mind, providing a welcome hobby and helping with stress for those on longer space missions.

132 WHO'S SPENT THE MOST TIME IN SPACE?

Russian Gennady Ivanovich Padalka holds the world record for the most time spent in space by a human—just over 878 days spanning five missions. Before taking off for the fifth time in March 2015, he declared his intention to return to space in the future to try and make it to 1,000 days, but it wasn't to be. He announced his retirement in 2017.

RUSSIAN VETERANS

Padalka was selected for cosmonaut training in 1989, having risen to the rank of colonel in the Soviet Air Force. His first mission was in 1998, when he became one of the last cosmonauts to spend time on the *Mir* space station, preparing it for deactivation and de-orbit. He has now enjoyed four visits to the International Space Station, spending two of those tours as station commander, and carried out nine space walks. He was commanding the ISS in 2009 when the space shuttle *Endeavour* docked and unloaded its crew. The seven newcomers boosted the total number onboard to 13—the largest human gathering in space in one craft.

LIVE THE DREAM

If you have the cash to spare, you too could make space history by buying a stay in space. At a cost of somewhere around the $35 million mark, you could buy a ticket to the space station. Someone who knows the thrill of this extravagant holiday is Charles Simonyi. The American software billionaire has taken two two-week trips to space at a cost of $25 million and $35 million respectively.

Fellow Russian Valeri Polyakov holds the record for longest individual space flight, spending 438 days aboard the *Mir* space station between 1994 and 1995. Extended space trips are extremely hard on the body. Because there's no gravity, the muscles we use against Earth's gravitational force have little work to do, resulting in muscle atrophy. Astronauts face a decrease in bone density, too, because bone tissue breaks down faster than it builds up. There are also the extreme psychological challenges faced by those spending months—14, in Polyakov's case—in the confines of a space station.

THE NEW SPACE RACE

The Americans have a long way to go to match Padalka's record. The record is currently held by Peggy Whitson, who has spent just over 665 days in space.

Whitson's longest single spaceflight lasted 289 days. She was also the first woman to command the ISS and the oldest woman to blast off into space when she set out aged 57 on her most recent mission in 2016. She retired from NASA two years later. The agency's astronauts hold other records, too. James Voss and Susan Helms hold the joint record for the longest space walks, spending eight hours and 56 minutes outside the space shuttle *Discovery* and the ISS in 2001, while Franklin Chang-Diaz and Jerry Ross share the record for most trips to space, both having made seven spaceflights throughout their careers. And to top that off, as of 2020, the ISS has had 242 different visitors from 19 different countries. More have been American (152) than any other nationality.

133 CAN ASTRONAUTS DRINK ALCOHOL ON THE JOB?

For most of us, the thought of spending weeks trapped in a confined capsule in space is enough to drive us to drink, but the truth is, while alcohol is sent on space missions for experimental purposes, astronauts aren't allowed to drink it. Although that hasn't always been the case . . .

SHERRY BAD IDEA

When NASA launched *Skylab*, the world's first space station, in 1973, it almost became the first bar in space, too. Original menu planning for the astronauts included sherry, deemed to be the most stable type of wine because it is heated during processing. Paul Masson California Rare Cream Sherry was selected from taste tests and ordered for the mission. A flexible plastic pouch package with a built-in drinking tube was developed to house the booze. But it seemed public opinion was opposed to any wild space parties and NASA's alcohol program came to an abrupt end. *Skylab*'s manager listed a number of reasons for the change of heart, including the expectation of "continued criticism and ridicule . . . if such a beverage is provided."

RUSSIAN REBELS

The strict NASA rules mean that American astronauts have no place for alcohol on the International Space Station, whereas Russian cosmonauts have had a much more relaxed approach to booze on board. Since the earliest Russian spaceflights, and particularly on the *Mir* space station, alcohol was a key part of the crew's rations. Former *Mir* crew member Aleksandr Lazutkin said that cognac was recommended by doctors "to stimulate the cosmonauts' immune system."

QUIZ
THE UNIVERSE AND SPACE

If this section helped you expand your mind, now's the time to test what you've learned. And if you get stuck, don't panic. The truth is out there!

QUESTIONS:

1. When the Moon was formed, was it closer to Earth or farther away from Earth than it is now?

2. Which American president's daughter received a puppy that was the offspring of one of the space dogs in the Russian space program?

3. Earth is spinning at 200 miles per hour—true or false?

4. Did Einstein's brain weigh considerably more than the average male's?

5. Was it a Soviet or a U.S. spacecraft that first photographed the far side of the Moon?

6. There are over 500,000 pieces of debris in space orbiting Earth— true or false?

7. What alcoholic drink almost became part of the *Skylab* menu?

8. What was the Arecibo message: a message from aliens, a message to aliens, or a message to humans in space?

9. What was the first vegetable to be grown and eaten in space?

10. Record-holder Valeri Polyakov spent four continuous years in space—true or false?

Turn to page 249 for the answers.

QUIZ ANSWERS

WEATHER AND CLIMATE

1. False. They will always be different on a molecular level, despite looking the same.

2. The longer it takes the snowman to burn, the longer winter will be.

3. Australia.

4. Stridulation.

5. Nor'easter, *purga*, *metel*, *v'yuga*, *buran*.

6. True.

7. Slower.

8. True.

9. Bangladesh.

10. Hurricanes.

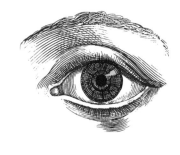

THE HUMAN BODY

1. Little bean.

2. Rabies.

3. Tickly cough, dementia, cancer, diabetes.

4. Their own way of talking.

5. Urine.

6. True.

7. False. Green is the rarest.

8. True—as much as 7% in some cases.

9. Red and white (and sometimes blue, too).

10. An Indian healer known as Sushruta recorded the first cosmetic surgeries at some point between 1000 and 600 BC.

ART AND ARCHITECTURE

1. False. It was for his third wife, Mumtaz Mahal.

2. The Eiffel Tower.

3. The seven continents.

4. True.

5. His right ear.

6. It's too far away. The Moon is 238,855 miles from our planet.

7. Duck eggs.

8. Campbell's.

9. False. It's based on David from the biblical story of David and Goliath.

10. Mexico.

ANIMALS AND PLANTS

1. Giraffe.

2. Its painful sting.

3. False. It's found in a dog's nose and is also known as the vomeronasal organ.

4. The blue whale.

5. Parrot.

6. True.

7. Large. The size of their brain in relation to their body is second only to humans.

8. Their diet of algae and shrimp.

9. True.

10. Leonie.

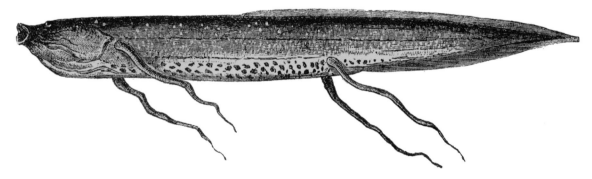

ANCIENT HISTORY

1. Kayaking.

2. False. There was a white granite quarry at the top of the mountain.

3. To build up immunity to poisons, due to the threat of assassination.

4. A famous document. The Magna Carta established important principles in English law in the 13th century.

5. More than 100 Olympic-size swimming pools.

6. Their heads and their teeth.

7. The tomb of China's first emperor, Qin Shi Huang, in Shaanxi Province.

8. False. They were entitled to one-third of it.

9. The Aztecs (or Mexica).

10. Being soldiers.

FOOD AND DRINK

1. More at risk.

2. Tea—2.35 trillion cups are produced every year, compared to 850 billion cups of coffee.

3. Lobster.

4. False. A *salarium* was a soldier's salary.

5. Chiclets chewing gum.

6. United States.

7. Chilies.

8. Parmigiano-Reggiano.

9. True.

10. The pig.

LITERATURE

1. A gray shawl.

2. Cadbury.

3. The *Harry Potter* books by
   J.K. Rowling.

4. Mark Twain.

5. Klingon.

6. Spy for the U.S. government.

7. Butterflies.

8. Oxford University Press.

9. True.

10. False. He was named after a black
    bear named "Winnipeg" and a toy
    swan named "Pooh."

GEOGRAPHY

1. Antarctica.

2. True.

3. Peru.

4. James Cameron.

5. The Amazon.

6. Mount Everest.

7. Montana, Wyoming,
   and Idaho.

8. Canada.

9. The Bermuda Triangle.

10. True.

SPORTS

1. True.

2. Waffles.

3. The bull's-eye.

4. Tidal bores.

5. 1936.

6. Jumping with a parachute from a low altitude, such as off a building or cliff.

7. False. They were introduced after research showed they were more visible to television audiences.

8. Mops.

9. To dig his own starting blocks.

10. False. They wear a yellow jersey. The polka-dot jersey is worn by the rider with the best climber ranking.

SCIENCE

1. Brown.

2. True, it is technically a lake.

3. Slows down.

4. Salty, sweet, sour, bitter, and umani.

5. False. There is no evidence to suggest this. However, it's believed yawning helps cool down the brain.

6. Dark chocolate, because of the higher concentrations of theobromine.

7. The Third Reich, run by the Nazis.

8. No. Four elements were added in 2015, with more yet to be discovered.

9. Khodinhi.

10. False. Luminol can help show where blood, bleach, and even horseradish have been, but not ketchup.

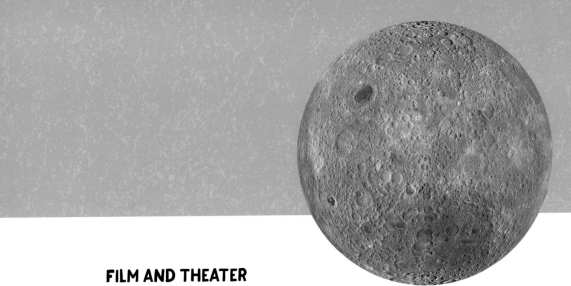

FILM AND THEATER

1. False. But he was paid more than the actors playing the Munchkins.

2. Teenage boys.

3. *Henry VIII.*

4. Paris.

5. Nollywood.

6. *Dragon.*

7. True.

8. Act.

9. False.

10. True.

THE UNIVERSE AND SPACE

1. It was closer to Earth.

2. John F. Kennedy's daughter.

3. False. It's actually spinning at 1,040 miles per hour.

4. No. In fact, it weighed toward the lower end of the normal range for a man of his age.

5. A Soviet spacecraft: *Luna 3.*

6. True.

7. Sherry.

8. A message to aliens. It was a 1974 transmission sent to 300,000 stars in the hope of contacting other intelligent life-forms.

9. Romaine lettuce.

10. False. But he has spent 438 consecutive days there.

INDEX

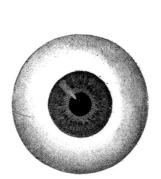
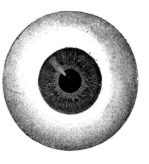

CREDITS

1, 3, 11, 31, 53, 71, 95, 113, 131, 151, 167, 185, 201, 223 © George Nikaragua | Shutterstock • 1, 3, 33, 188 © Alexander P | Shutterstock • 6, 52, 61 © Luciano Mortula | Shutterstock 7, 17, 32, 53, 54, 64, 66, 70, 71, 87, 88, 89, 94, 98, 99, 101, 102, 103, 130, 132, 144, 157, 200, 233, 235, 241 wikimedia.org • 7 © GeorgePeters | iStock • 7, 166 © DEL Studio | Shutterstock 7, 237 © Galaticus | Shutterstock • 7, 82 © GreyGoose Gosling | iStock • 7, 106 © Christos Georghiou | Shutterstock • 8, 13, 204 © lestyan | Shutterstock • 8 © Dita | Shutterstock • 8 © localdoctor | Shutterstock • 8 © Kseniakrop | Shutterstock • 8, 30, 39, 42, 70, 73, 193, 228 © Hein Nouwens | Shutterstock • 8 © mart | Shutterstock 10 © Vector FX | Shutterstock • 10, 18, 23 © Melock | Shutterstock • 10, 25 © Pink Pueblo | Shutterstock • 12 © DiViArt | Shutterstock • 13, 44, 46, 50, 59, 95, 98, 109, 128, 188, 209, 213, 215, 233 © Morphart Creation | Shutterstock • 14 © anussa | Shutterstock • 15, 45, 65, 85, 107, 117, 135, 155, 179, 201, 211, 231 © Graphicsfairy • 1, 3, 15, 45, 67, 85, 107, 117, 135, 155, 179, 201, 211, 231 © Ashley van Dyke | Shutterstock • 19 © cdstocks | Shutterstock • 20 © Antonpix | Shutterstock • 21 © chempina | Shutterstock • 24 © lynea | Shutterstock • 30, 91 © Betacam | Shutterstock • 31, 38 © Prokhorovich | Shutterstock • 34 © Maisei Raman | Shutterstock • 35 © SciePro | Shutterstock • 40 © Melica | Shutterstock • 40 © adehoidar | Shutterstock • 47, 48, 49, 190 © Wellcome Images • 52, 55 © Aleks Melnik | Shutterstock • 52, 63 © muratart | Shutterstock • 52, 62 © mashuk | istock • 53 © Giuliano del Moretto | Shutterstock • 56 © The Protected Art Archive | Alamy Stock Photo, Vector Tradition SM | Shutterstock • 57 © charl898 | Shutterstock • 63 © svetjekolem | Shutterstock 65 © Baurz1973 | Shutterstock • 68 © Andrew Unangst | Alamy Stock Photo • 70, 77 © ibusca | iStock • 72 © Patrick K. Campbell | Shutterstock • 75, 120, 200, 255 © INTERFOTO | Alamy Stock Photo • 76 © Eric Isselee | Shutterstock • 78 © Jolygon | Shutterstock • 79 © Florilegius | Alamy • 80 © Jollanda | Shutterstock • 81 © Stocksnapper | Shutterstock, Real PIX | Shutterstock • 83 © ArchMan | Shutterstock. Robert Adrian Hillman | Shutterstock • 84 © cynoclub | iStock • 91 © Coprid | Shutterstock • 92 © Marzolino | Shutterstock • 94, 97 © Ian Dyball | Shutterstock • • 96 © flocu | Shutterstock • 103 © testing |

Shutterstock • 104 © Stocksnapper | Shutterstock •105 © Voropaev Vasiliy | Shutterstock • 108 © Anastasios71 | Shutterstock • 110 © Jjustas | Shutterstock, Sofiaworld | Shutterstock • 112, 124 © Maryna Kulchytska | Shutterstock • 112, 114 © GeorgePeters | iStock • 112 © 96 © Tatiana Ivleva | Shutterstock • 112, 122 © epine | Shutterstock • 113, 123 © Maisei Raman | Shutterstock • 115 © lynea | Shutterstock • 116 © ppi09 | Shutterstock • 118 © Shaliapina | Shutterstock • 119 © CSA Images | iStock • 120 © Anatoly Shapoval | Shutterstock • 121 © Alvaro German Vilela | Shutterstock • 96 © flocu | Shutterstock • 124 © andrey oleynik | Shutterstock • • 126 © MoreVector | Shutterstock • 126 © Hekla | Shutterstock • 130, 148 © Dita | Shutterstock • 130, 141 © Ryger | Shutterstock • 130, 139 © Sunny Designs | Shutterstock • 33 © Drozhzhina Elena | Shutterstock • 134 © newelle | Shutterstock • 136 © Schwabenblitz | Shutterstock • 137 © Babich Alexander | Shutterstock • 138, 208, 212 © Everett Collection | Shutterstock • 140 © ilbusca | iStock • 143 © Bodor Tivadar | Shutterstock • 145 © rob zs | Shutterstock • 146 © Everett Collection Historical | Alamy Stock Photo • 147 © benoitb | iStock • 150, 160 © Danussa | Shutterstock • 150, 164 © Alex Rockheart | Shutterstock • 154 © Rainer Lesniewski | Shutterstock •156, 161 © skelos | Shutterstock • 158 © Mystical Link | Shutterstock • 159, 171, 177, 220 © Getty Images • 163 © Nasbka | Shutterstock • 166 © isaxar | Shutterstock • 163, 182 © Nasbka | Shutterstock • 163, 180 © Sarfev | Shutterstock • 168 © Alamay • 163 © Nasbka | Shutterstock • 173 © gomolach | Shutterstock • 174 © RetroClipArt | Shutterstock • 175 © Haelen Haagen | Shutterstock • 176 © Aaron Amat | Shutterstock • 187 © JONGSUK | Shutterstock • 188 © Good Studio | Shutterstock • 196 © an_Half–tube | iStock • 199 © alexandre zveiger | Shutterstock • 199 © Gregory Gerber | Shutterstock • 210 © BernardAllum | iStock • 212 © mariia kalinina | Shutterstock • 214 © andersphoto | Shutterstock • • 216 © zu_09 | istock • 216 © wpap | Shutterstock • 218 © Marzolino | Shutterstock • 219 © FrimuFilms | Shutterstock • 224 © AstroStar | Shutterstock • 225 © Danussa | Shutterstock • 226 © Tairy Greene | Shutterstock • 227 © Heritage Image Partnership Ltd | Alamy Stock Photo • 238 © koko adi p | Shutterstock • 242 © studiostoks | Shutterstock •Shutterstock